SMALL PET HEALTH CARE AND BREEDING

Susan Fox

Photo credits: Glen S. Axelrod, Joan Balzarini, Bob Bernhard, Bonnie Buys, Susan Fox, Isabelle Francais, Peter Gurney, Michael Gilroy, Ralph Lermayer, Horst Mayer, Daniel R. Schwartz, DVM, John Tyson, Louise B. van der Meid, Terry Wing, John A. Zeinert

© T.F.H. Publications, Inc.

Distributed in the UNITED STATES to the Pet Trade by T.F.H. Publications, Inc., 1 TFH Plaza, Neptune City, NJ 07753; on the Internet at www.tfh.com; in CANADA by Rolf C. Hagen Inc., 3225 Sartelon St., Montreal, Quebec H4R 1E8; Pet Trade by H & L Pet Supplies Inc., 27 Kingston Crescent, Kitchener, Ontario N2B 2T6; in ENGLAND by T.F.H. Publications, PO Box 74, Havant PO9 5TT; in AUSTRALIA AND THE SOUTH PACIFIC by T.F.H. (Australia), Pty. Ltd., Box 149, Brookvale 2100 N.S.W., Australia; in NEW ZEALAND by Brooklands Aquarium Ltd., 5 McGiven Drive, New Plymouth, RD1 New Zealand; in SOUTH AFRICA by Rolf C. Hagen S.A. (PTY.) LTD., P.O. Box 201199, Durban North 4016, South Africa; in JAPAN by T.F.H. Publications. Published by T.F.H. Publications, Inc.

MANUFACTURED IN THE
UNITED STATES OF AMERICA
BY T.F.H. PUBLICATIONS, INC.

CONTENTS

INTRODUCTION

My first pet was a guinea pig. My father brought it home after much asking—actually, incessant begging. A friend who raised cavies told me they needed vitamin C and sunshine for vitamin D activity. That was pretty much all the knowledge I received. Much has changed in our ability to diagnose and treat our small furry pets. "Cage enrichment" and MRI were unheard of at that time. Veterinary students today, however, expect to be trained in the medicine and surgery of non-traditional pets.

Exotic animal medicine can now provide all the tools available for dogs, cats, and people, including ultrasound, CAT scans, chemo and radiation therapies, and advanced anesthesia and surgical

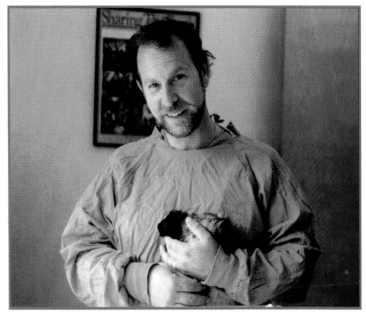

This book has been thoroughly reviewed for accuracy by the author of the introduction, veterinarian R. Brooks Bloomfield, DVM.

care. Money is the most limiting factor in small mammal medicine today. It

When you call your veterinarian for help with non-traditional pets, you'll likely find a willing partner in the care of your pet. Veterinarians today are more adept at treating small mammals than ever before.

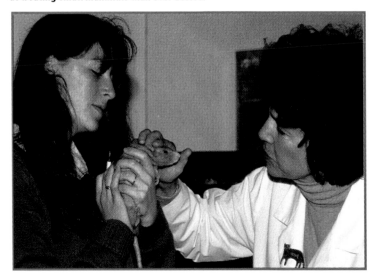

is not always practical or even reasonable to spend hundreds of dollars on a family pet that has a limited life span or grave prognosis. Remember that small mammal medicine is often more delicate, dangerous, and both time and labor-intensive than traditional pet medicine. Usually though, pets treated promptly are also treated affordably and effectively.

Call your veterinarian for help with non-traditional pets. You'll likely find a willing partner in the care of your pet—someone with intense curiosity who will work hard to diagnose your pet and guide you in its care.

—R. Brooks Bloomfield, DVM

EVOLVING MEDICINE

In the past, pet stores traditionally served as valuable sources of information about the health care of small fuzzy pets such as rodents. Pet store owners and their employees often reared these animals and were more familiar with their husbandry and potential ailments than many veterinarians were. In many cases, veterinarians were not trained in the health care of these small pets. Some veterinarians viewed pet rodents and rabbits as laboratory animals and failed to appreciate their status as pets. This bias was sometimes communicated to the pet owners, who turned to pet store personnel for more understanding.

In the last dozen years, much has changed in the field of small animal medicine. Most veterinarians are now qualified to treat small pets' ailments and have the sensitivity to address owners' concerns. Several factors have contributed to this change. More veterinary students are exposed to small mammals as part of their training rotation, and thus more graduates have the knowledge to treat non-traditional pets.

Small pet owners now expect the same quality of care for their pets that they receive for other types of animals, such as birds and dogs. More people keeping small fuzzy pets created an economic demand for the animals' proper health care. Veterinarians are able to more effectively treat these pets because they have the methods, equipment, and facilities (e.g., small-gauge needles for intravenous fluids and warm cages for small pets to recuperate in from surgery). In addition, just as technologies such as ultrasound that are used for human illnesses are available for use in pets such as dogs, they can also be used for small pets.

In the past, pet stores like this one were the most valuable source of information about the health care of small mammals. Many veterinarians were not trained or equipped to treat small pets.

It is now more expected for veterinarians to see and treat small pets. The medical diagnoses of conditions affecting these pets are more familiar to many practitioners. As increasing numbers of pets are seen, a more reliable picture of what is "normal" has developed.

Excellent reference texts devoted to the treatment of small fuzzy pets are available. Besides descriptions of diseases, these manuals contain information such as known drug dosages, medications that are toxic to certain species, and

Much of the information historically available about the health care of small pets came from places such as this commercial breeding facility. Although much of this information is applicable to animals kept as pets, some is not.

In the last few years, much has changed in the field of small animal medicine. Most veterinarians are now qualified to treat small pets' ailments and have the sensitivity to address owners' concerns.

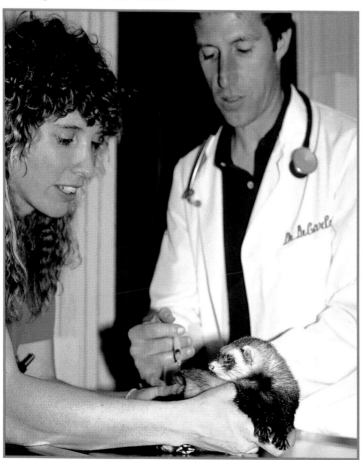

information on blood chemistry. However, even with all the medical advances, some ailments are so uncommon that accurate diagnosis is difficult, and even when the condition is known, there might be no effective treatment.

Veterinary medicine will continue to expand as more information accumulates regarding the ailments that affect small furry pets and the successful treatment of such conditions. Animal medicine has shown itself to be responsive to changes in pet ownership trends, because more veterinarians are now trained to treat small furry pets. Knowledge is even growing of the health and diseases of many of the newer exotic pets, such as hedgehogs, prairie dogs, and sugar gliders. If you take your pet to a veterinarian, there is a better chance of an accurate diagnosis and a better outcome if the condition is treatable. The outlook will only get better as veterinarians attracted by the

The concerns of a pet owner are, of course, different from those of a researcher or commercial breeder. For example, this young owner is probably more interested in how friendly her hamster is than in the quality of his coat.

potential for original research further investigate the conditions affecting small fuzzy pets.

IN THE PAST

Much of the information available on the ailments of small mammals in the past came from places where the animals were not kept as pets, such as research facilities and fur farms. Although much of this information is applicable to

pets, some of it is not. Pet animals are susceptible to different illnesses than animals kept in other settings. For example, humans are the natural host for several types of *Streptococci* bacteria. These bacteria can adversely affect small animals when they are transmitted from people to susceptible pets. However, in a laboratory, the scientists do not necessarily come into direct contact with the

animals, which are often housed in a sterile environment where there is little risk of exposure. Conversely, however, ringtail, which results in a rat losing part or all of his tail due to low environmental humidity, is more commonly seen in rats kept in laboratories than as pets.

In addition, people who keep animals as pets have different concerns than scientists who use them in research and farmers who rear them for pelts. Disease processes are more likely to occur in pets allowed to live out their natural life span than in animals that are kept alive for only a short period of time. Pet owners might have to contend with problems such as obesity or trauma injuries (from a pet that has accidentally been dropped). They are less concerned if their pet's coat is not in prime condition, and in fact they might not even notice the condition of the coat.

Eager to avoid the cost of a veterinary bill unless their pet is very sick, pet owners often seek recommendations from pet store employees before taking their pet to a veterinarian. Although pet store employees might be helpful and able to give an educated guess about the ailment, the expertise, diagnostic skills, and medication needed to treat the pet are only available from a veterinarian. Pet stores also sell some products that can be used for illnesses, such as "wet tail" in hamsters. These treatments are options, but again, a prompt visit to the veterinarian is the best guarantee of a successful outcome and is usually very affordable.

Most small pets that are sick need to be treated by a veterinarian immediately. This is especially important because pet owners often do not notice symptoms in their pet until the animal is very ill. Small animals do not usually show signs of illness until late in the course of a disease. The ability to hide an illness is believed to be a self-protective behavior. In the wild, an animal that acts sick is easy prey for predators. By the time a pet owner realizes that an animal is ill, the pet has usually been sick for quite some time. In many cases, treatment is difficult because the condition is so advanced at the time of detection. Although some diseases progress rapidly—an affected

Before you buy a pet, decide if you will be willing to provide the necessary veterinary care.

pet can die in 24 hours or less—early recognition of a sick animal may mean the

difference between life and death for your pet.

Furthermore, keep in mind that the sicker a pet is, the more likely he is to be traumatized by the procedures at a veterinarian's office. For example, an animal with labored breathing might need to have an x-ray taken. Rarely, a pet that is this sick might die from the stress of being restrained during the x-ray.

FINDING A VETERINARIAN

In order for your pet to receive the proper treatment, the illness must be correctly diagnosed. A veterinarian who routinely treats small mammals and has a special interest in their care is best qualified and will most likely have the necessary, smaller-sized equipment. Such individuals are more likely to be aware of advances and changes in treatment protocol.

Veterinarians who specialize in small mammals can be easier to find in some areas of the country than in others (such as in urban areas compared with rural areas). In order to locate the right veterinarian, inquire at pet stores, small pet clubs, rescue societies (e.g., the House Rabbit Society), as well as at veterinarians' offices.

COST

Even when pet owners recognize that their animals are "under the weather," some hesitate to take their pet to a veterinarian because of the potential expense. It is often helpful to have decided beforehand whether you are willing to incur the cost of

A sick animal should visit the veterinarian as soon as possible, because treatment is always more difficult if the disease is very advanced.

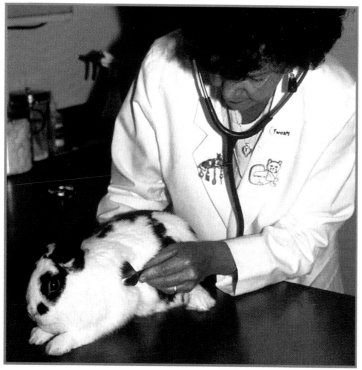

treatment. Plan on requiring vet care before you buy a pet. Some small pets are well-loved members of a family and the owners will pay for costly care. However, other pets are more "expendable" and will not receive treatment.

The cost of treating a small pet often seems disproportionate to the perceived value of the pet. It is just as costly to treat a rat for an illness as it is to treat a dog. The medical technology to diagnose conditions is the same, so therefore the cost is the same. Many small animal owners (or the parents of a child who has a small animal) find it difficult to spend large sums of money on a pet that only cost a few dollars. Even veterinarians often make "educated guesses" as to what ails the

The fact that veterinary care is just as expensive for a small mammal as it is for a dog surprises many pet owners. However, rodents and similar pets are smaller and more delicate (making surgery and medication a challenge) and the technology for diagnostic tests costs just as much.

By discussing potential costs with your veterinarian beforehand, you will be better able to plan your pet's treatment.

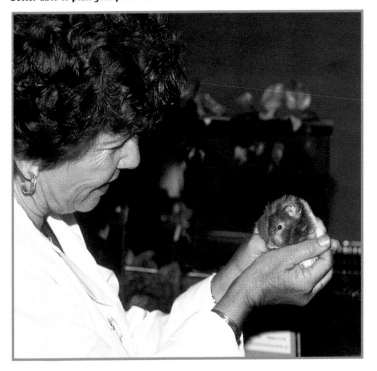

pet, because diagnostic tests are often cost-prohibitive.

Occasionally, pet owners feel their veterinarian is conspiring against them financially when he requests that they bring their pet in for a follow-up visit. Contrary to their suspicions, many illnesses do require a follow-up to assess how well the pet is responding to the treatment. By discussing potential costs with your veterinarian beforehand, you will have a better idea of how much your pet's care might cost. Although it might be difficult to put a price on your beloved pet, in some cases, this might be necessary so you can decide how much you can afford to spend. If necessary, check whether your veterinarian has payment plan options available.

HEALTH CARE OF YOUR SMALL PET

Sick small animals generally present with a similar range of signs and symptoms. Obvious signs of illness include discharge from the eyes or nose.

Because small animals are fastidious about keeping themselves clean, the discharge is often visible on their paws from their grooming efforts.

Sudden changes in behavior, such as lethargy and reduced appetite, also indicate illness. Signs of disease that are more difficult to detect include rough hair, hunched posture, and weight loss. A pet's behavior might also change. Instead of frolicking in his cage or running on his exercise wheel like he

normally would, he might huddle in a corner. Sometimes a pet's temperament changes, and a friendly animal becomes aggressive. Particular attention should be paid if a

pet is sensitive to being touched on a certain part of his body. Any of these signs suggest that something might be wrong with the animal and that a visit to the veterinarian might be prudent.

Ferrets are the only small pets that are seen by veterinarians for regular annual appointments.

Sick small animals like this rabbit frequently display obvious signs of illness such as discharge from the eyes or nose.

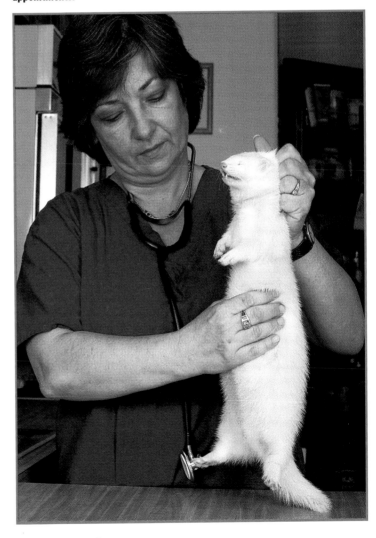

With the exception of ferrets, small pets are not usually seen by veterinarians annually. Therefore, there is no opportunity for early detection of some problems. By familiarizing yourself with the signs of various ailments, you may be better prepared to recognize if your pet is sick and to communicate his symptoms to your veterinarian.

Be prepared also to describe your pet's housing and feeding regimes. Sometimes, a veterinarian might request that you bring your pet in with his cage or bring a photograph of the cage setup so that the pet's environment can be assessed. (Otherwise, you will need a secure box or carrier cage,

Many of the symptoms of sick small mammals are subtle—would you be able to tell if this rat had a headache?

like those available at pet stores, to take your pet to the veterinarian.)

It is often obvious to people when another person is sick, perhaps because they

When you bring your pet to the vet's office, you will need a secure box or carrier cage like this one.

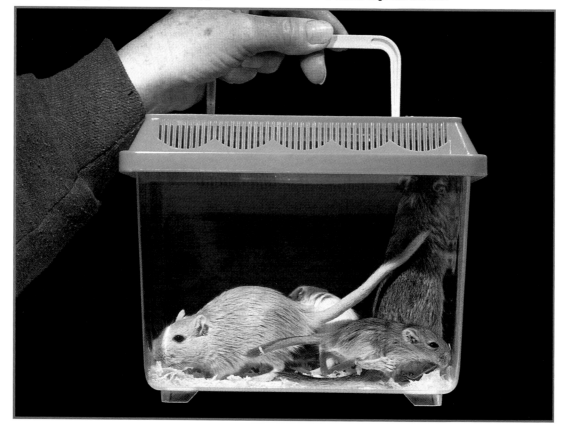

themselves have experienced similar symptoms from an illness, such as a cough due to a cold. However, unless someone *states* that they have a splitting headache, such an ailment can be more difficult to detect. Like a headache, many of the symptoms of sick small mammals are subtle, and a pet's facial expression certainly does not give any indication of his state of health. Experienced pet owners and breeders are adept at recognizing when a pet is sick. As you gain experience in caring for your pet, especially if you develop a long-term interest, you will also become more proficient.

Stress is a major cause of illness, and overcrowding is frequently a cause of stress.

WHAT IS STRESS?

Stress is a catch-all word for a variety of conditions that disturb or interfere with a pet's normal physiological equilibrium. Because stress often leads to illness, it is frequently mentioned as a detrimental, contributing factor to various diseases. Besides becoming sick, a pet can exhibit signs of stress in

The trip from a pet store or breeder's house to a new home can also be a cause of stress and illness. It is important to give a new pet plenty of time to settle in before handling him or introducing him to other pets.

other ways, such as irritability, repetitive movements, lack of appetite, hair loss, and loose droppings. It is useful for pet owners to be aware of what constitutes stress for their pets.

An animal can experience stress from pain and fear, when moving to a new cage, from a change in diet, exposure to temperature fluctuations, and so forth. Some species and some individuals tolerate stressful situations better than others. For example, rabbits and chinchillas are very sensitive to heat stroke. For these animals, any trip to the veterinarian is stressful, but during hot weather, a trip in a car without air conditioning can be very dangerous. While temperature changes are always undesirable, some animals, such as rats, are comparatively better able to tolerate these variations.

Other stressful situations include weaning, loud noises, when a female is nursing her litter, and overcrowding. The behavior of animals that share a cage must be taken into account. Groups of small animals housed together can fight and injure each other. Fighting and bullying is particularly stressful for the animal that is always picked on because he is at the bottom of the pecking order. Owners should protect vulnerable animals from more aggressive individuals—for example, young animals from older ones or males from unreceptive females. Often, such situations must be resolved by moving some individuals to separate cages. (Keep in mind that small animals such as mice, hamsters, and gerbils often fight at night, when you are not awake to see or hear them.)

The trip from a pet store or breeder to a new home can be frightening and stressful for many animals. Once in their new environment, some animals settle down right away, while others take longer to adjust.

Stress can be a major factor in the development of what might otherwise remain a dormant disease. Therefore, it is wise to minimize the stress in a pet's life.

TYPES OF HEALTH PROBLEMS

When purchased from a reliable source and given good care, the typical small pet is hardy and resilient. However, even with the best precautionary measures, a pet might still become ill. It is useful and even interesting to become familiar with some of the more common types of illness that can affect small animals. Of course, your pet is not likely to get many of the

ailments described, but learning about the causes of these illnesses might help you prevent your pet from getting sick.

The ailments that affect small animals can be classified into six categories: (1) traumatic injuries, (2) infectious diseases, (3) noninfectious diseases, (4) ailments caused by improper husbandry, (5) hereditary diseases, and (6) problems related to nutrition and aging. The reasons that an animal becomes sick are often a combination of factors from more than one category. For example, a poorly ventilated cage can create a noxious-smelling environment with high levels of ammonia, causing a recurrence of a latent respiratory disease. Numerous factors will affect how sick the animal will get. These factors include the virulence of the pathogen, the

animal's age, dietary deficiencies, and whether the animal is already sick with another illness (e.g., diabetes). Illness from organ failure depends on the cause and extent of organ damage.

Traumatic Injuries

When an animal has a traumatic injury, it is usually obvious. The pet is often in acute and immediate pain and distress, and the pet owner often knows why—for example, the pet fell, was dropped, or was squeezed. Trauma is easier to treat than infectious diseases because it is easier to detect. If an animal breaks a leg, the pet owner usually brings it in right away for veterinary care.

While all types of small animal are subject to traumatic injuries, the kind of injury often depends on the type of pet. Small animals, such as hamsters and gerbils,

Common traumatic injuries vary depending on the size of the pet. Tiny hamsters and gerbils tend to be squeezed too hard, whereas larger guinea pigs and rabbits are more frequently dropped accidentally.

are more likely to be squeezed, whereas larger pets, such as guinea pigs and rabbits, are more likely to be dropped and receive broken bones. Knowing how to hold and play with a pet properly can prevent such injuries from occurring.

Never self-medicate your pets with antibiotics, because many species are extremely sensitive to their effects. The wrong drug—or the right drug at the wrong dose—can easily kill a small pet.

Infectious Diseases

Infectious diseases can spread from one animal to another and are caused by bacteria, viruses, fungi, and protozoans. Sometimes, the diseases caused by these agents are subclinical, with the signs of infection difficult to detect. Individual animals also differ in their resistance to infectious organisms. Some exposed animals never display any symptoms. However, stress or other bacterial or viral infections can cause an animal to show symptoms suddenly. A single pet is less at risk for infectious diseases than a pet that is housed in close proximity to large numbers of other animals of the same species. Infectious diseases are often preventable through good husbandry.

Compared to traumatic injuries, infectious diseases are often more difficult to detect. Initial symptoms are often overlooked, especially if the pet is played with infrequently or if he belongs to a young child. Pet owners usually do not recognize symptoms that could indicate an illness. A pet might not eat his regular ration one day and gradually exhibit a decreased appetite, but many pet owners have a tendency to minimize the importance of such signs. A pet owner typically brings an animal to the veterinarian after many days have passed

and when other problems such as weight loss and lethargy have developed. By that time, it is often too late for effective treatment.

Some infectious diseases that are caused by bacteria are treated with antibiotics. After reading about an antibiotic that is effective against the illness they think their pet might have, some pet owners who are anxious to avoid the expense of veterinary bills buy antibiotics from the fish or bird section of a pet store. Naturally, this is not recommended. Treatments change over time, and it is highly unlikely that the pet will actually receive an effective dose of the

appropriate antibiotic. For example, tetracycline used to be the treatment of choice for murine respiratory disease syndrome, which causes sniffles and sneezing in rats. This is no longer the case. Moreover, the use of an unprescribed antibiotic can kill the animal or complicate future diagnostic efforts if the owner decides to take the pet to a veterinarian.

Some species of small pet are very sensitive to the effects of certain antibiotics. Antibiotics can kill small animals because they alter the useful bacteria that normally live in the animal's digestive system (sometimes referred to as "good" bacteria

Infectious diseases easily spread from one animal to others sharing the cage.

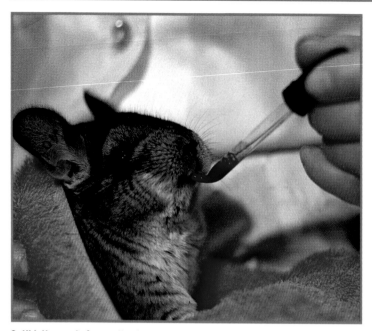

Antibiotics made for small pets are usually in the form of a tasty syrup.

enough to completely eliminate the pathogen. In addition, the illness your pet has might not be curable with an antibiotic.

Antibiotics provided for small pets by a veterinarian are often in a palatable syrup, while fish and bird medications must be dissolved in drinking water. Many animals find this distasteful and will not drink the water even when it is sweetened.

Products sold in pet stores *specifically* for use in small fuzzy pets can generally be regarded as safe, though their effectiveness cannot be predicted.

Noninfectious Diseases

Noninfectious diseases include a variety of conditions that are not typically transmitted from one animal to another. Tumors, which are a form of cancer, are one type of noninfectious disease. They are seldom seen in the young animals offered for sale in pet stores. More often, tumors occur in middle-aged and older animals. When playing with your pet, you might notice a swelling under the skin, which could be a tumor or abscess. If your pet has a lump, you should consult a veterinarian to determine whether it is a tumor and whether surgery is recommended. Some tumors, however, occur internally and are not easily detected by a pet owner.

An abscess is usually caused by a bacterial infection from a wound inflicted during a fight, or it could be caused by an infection from a cut. A veterinarian must tend to an abscess. Using a needle, the

or "gut flora"). Small mammals such as rabbits and hamsters digest their food by a process called fermentation. They need their intestinal bacteria for proper digestion because the bacteria help to convert food into a form that the animal can use. These microscopic organisms are essential to the animal's health and perform important functions such as the synthesis of vitamins.

The animal is not usually sensitive to the drug as much as he is susceptible to the effects of the antibiotic on the natural intestinal flora. The wrong antibiotic can completely destroy the good bacteria, which can lead to the animal's death. Some antibiotics allow harmful bacteria to grow. These noxious bacteria produce toxins that then kill the pet. Because of these risks, antibiotic therapy in small fuzzy pets must be carefully monitored for possible

adverse effects by the pet owner, in conjunction with a veterinarian. Veterinary manuals contain recommended dosages for antibiotics and list which types can be safely used for each species and for which conditions. In many cases, new antibiotics have been developed that prevent harmful side effects.

This sensitivity is just one reason why buying antibiotics sold for fish or birds in pet stores is not recommended. Besides the possibility of using the wrong antibiotic, a small furry pet can be done more harm than good if the dose is too high or too low. Even when using an appropriate medication, it can be difficult to provide a nonprescribed antibiotic at the right dose. At first, your pet might seem to respond, but there is a good chance that he will exhibit recurrent symptoms because the treatment does not last long veterinarian will aspirate (or sample) the abscess, then drain and clean the site. In some species, the abscesses must be removed instead of drained. Usually, an oral antibiotic is prescribed. The bacteria that cause an abscess are often opportunistic and can infect other organs besides the skin. It is important that an affected pet be properly treated. A veterinarian might deem it necessary to culture, or grow, a sample of the fluid to identify the type of bacteria present. An antibiotic selected on the basis of culture and sensitivity test results is likely to be highly effective.

Because infection from bacteria is always possible when an animal is bitten in a fight, clean any injuries with warm water and an antiseptic. Watch the wounds, and if you detect any prolonged swelling

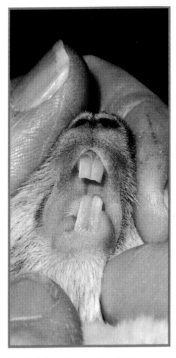

The bright yellow color of this chinchilla's teeth is normal, and they are properly aligned.

or other signs of illness, take the animal to the veterinarian.

Teeth—Rodents and rabbits have chisel-like incisors in the front of their mouths. (Rodents have four incisor teeth, while rabbits, which are classified as lagomorphs, have six—two pairs in the upper jaw and one pair in the lower jaw.) These teeth never stop growing, and in some species, they can grow up to five inches in a year. Teeth that continuously grow are termed "open-root," in contrast to "closed-root" teeth, which do not continuously grow. The incisors are worn down by the animal's gnawing and chewing on hard substances.

In addition to the incisors, the molar teeth of rabbits, guinea pigs, and chinchillas also continue to grow throughout their lives.

This ferret is recovering from an abscess that has been removed and drained. A veterinarian has prescribed an oral antibiotic to clear up the infection.

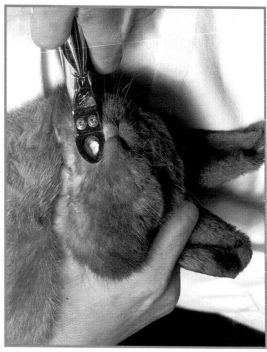

The rabbit's teeth at left are broken and maloccluded. At right, a veterinarian carefully trims them so they are even again.

The teeth of small fuzzy pets sometimes need veterinary attention because of malocclusion. Malocclusion occurs when an animal's teeth do not meet properly, either because the teeth are overgrown or because they are misaligned. In some pets, such as rabbits, malocclusion is one of the more common reasons people bring their pets to veterinarians. An animal's teeth can fail to meet and wear properly for several reasons. Malocclusion may be inherited, or it may be caused by trauma, infection, or improper diet (i.e., the pet does not regularly eat foods hard enough to wear down his teeth).

Animals with this condition eventually cannot eat, lose weight, and will die without treatment. Many show a symptom referred to as the "slobbers," which are threads of saliva around the mouth that are sometimes wiped on the front paws. A secondary sign of molar malocclusion in rabbits and guinea pigs is droppings containing large pieces of undigested food, because the animal cannot chew properly. If you notice that your pet is not eating, you can check his incisors by pulling back his lips, but a veterinarian must usually diagnose malocclusion of the molars.

Either way, an affected animal must be taken to a veterinarian. When left untreated, malocclusion can cause some gruesome results, such as the incisors growing into the animal's nasal cavity or the molars lacerating the tongue and soft inside cheeks, potentially causing abscesses. Overgrown incisors are seen most frequently in rats and mice, while molar malocclusion is observed most often in guinea pigs and chinchillas.

Overgrown incisors are easily treated by a veterinarian. While the animal is still conscious, the vet can clip the overgrown teeth. However, this procedure sometimes does not produce good results and can cause other problems to develop. This method can cause an incisor to split, fracture, or have jagged edges. If the tooth splinters all the way to the gum, it not only will cause the animal pain, it might also allow bacteria to enter the tooth and cause an abscess in the tooth's root. When clipped teeth are left with jagged edges, the inside of the animal's mouth and his tongue might be cut by the rough edges, causing discomfort and possible sites for infection.

This is an uncommon complication, but to prevent such problems, some veterinarians prefer to use a high-speed drill. The drill leaves a smooth surface while cutting through the overgrown incisors without splitting or fracturing them. The only potential drawback is that your pet may need to be sedated for this procedure.

As an alternative to constantly trimming overgrown incisors, your veterinarian might discuss the possibility of extracting these teeth. However, because of the incisors' long roots, this process is sometimes difficult to perform successfully.

Pets that need to have their overgrown molars treated must first be anesthetized. Specially designed veterinary tools help to open an animal's mouth and keep it open so that molar teeth can be appropriately filed with a rasp.

Many animal care books recommend that an animal's teeth be inspected before buying him. However, be aware that *hereditary* malocclusion is often not detectable in young animals. Even if the teeth appear normal at first, as the animal matures, unfavorable changes can occur. Responsible breeders will not breed from individuals that develop malocclusion, so ideally the

incidence of hereditary malocclusion will diminish.

Unlike rodents and rabbits, ferrets, which are mustelids, have closed-root teeth that do not continuously grow. While a ferret's teeth might not need to be trimmed, they can accumulate plaque that calcifies, forming tartar, like that on a cat or dog's teeth. Tartar under the gumline can cause irritation and infection and must be removed. A veterinarian can check and clean your ferret's teeth as part of his regular check-up. However, for a thorough cleaning, the ferret must be anesthetized. Between visits to the veterinarian and when necessary, some ferret owners learn to clean their pet's teeth themselves using teeth cleaning instruments. Ferret-

sized toothbrushes are available as well as specially formulated enzymatic toothpaste.

As part of your pet's general care, it is important that you are comfortable checking your pet's teeth on occasion. If this is intimidating, ask your veterinarian to show you how to do so. Healthy teeth are important for all small mammal pets. When dental conditions are left untreated, more serious problems such as gum disease, tooth loss, and kidney infection can develop.

Ears—Small animals can get ear mites and ear infections. If left untreated, these infestations can cause serious problems. Take your pet to a veterinarian if you

Ferrets' teeth do not grow continuously as those of rodents and rabbits do. Because of this, ferrets have the same problems with plaque and tartar as cats, dogs, and humans. Periodic dental cleanings will prevent tooth decay.

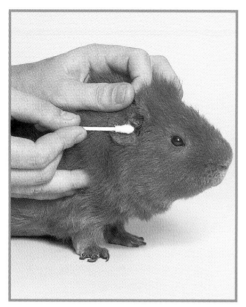
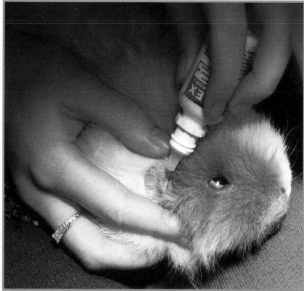

Pet owners should clean their pets' ears gently with a moist cotton swab (left) and medicate for ear mites and infections when necessary (right).

notice excessive scratching, heavy wax buildup, discharge, or a growth. The most effective treatment and advice on remedying the problem is available from a veterinarian. Do not automatically assume any discharge is from ear mites and treat with an ear mite medication sold at pet stores. Accurate diagnosis of the condition will speed your pet's recovery and save him from discomfort and pain. Owners of ferrets and rabbits should examine their pets' ears every few weeks. They can gently clean their pets' outer ears with a cotton swab and a veterinary ear cleanser. The wax in the external ear should be carefully removed, without going into the ear canal.

Skin and Fur—Small animals are naturally clean. They spend up to 20 percent of their waking hours grooming themselves. Even rats spend a lot of time washing themselves; delicately cleaning each ear with their toes, then cleaning their toes with their tongue, washing their front and backside, and even scrubbing their long tails. A small animal that cannot keep himself clean is probably sick and should be examined by a veterinarian.

Rabbits, guinea pigs, and ferrets are the only small animals that shed any noticeable hair, especially when they molt. Long-haired breeds of rabbit (e.g., angoras) and guinea pigs (e.g., Peruvians) need daily brushing and regular trimming of their long coats. A rubber brush can be used to groom these pets each day.

It's easy to see why long-haired breeds of rabbit like this English Angora need to be brushed daily—their coats can be hard to manage for the novice owner.

Short-haired varieties do not need to be groomed, but many animals enjoy being brushed with a soft brush or toothbrush. Other small animals, such as hamsters, gerbils, and mice, do not need to have their coats brushed. However, if the pets will hold still, some owners of these animals like to brush them with a soft toothbrush.

Grooming sessions are a good time to notice whether a pet has a rough coat, dry or flaky skin, lumps, scabs, or evidence of external parasites, such as flea dirt. Pet stores sell specific products that are safe to use on external parasites for some species of small mammal, such as ferrets. However, it might be necessary for your veterinarian to prescribe an appropriate treatment for external parasites such as mites on other species of small mammals. Skin scrapings or skin biopsies are the usual way to diagnose external parasites. Some of the parasites that infect small mammals do infect people, and they can infect other small pets as well. Therefore, an infected pet should be isolated, and you should wash your hands after handling and treating a pet that has parasites.

Hairballs can present problems in ferrets, rabbits, and long-haired guinea pigs. Animals sometimes swallow a lot of hair when they groom themselves, especially during a molt. Unlike cats, rabbits cannot vomit up hairballs. If untreated, hairballs can cause intestinal blockage and even death. Symptoms typically include lethargy, lack of appetite, weight loss,

While it is not necessary to brush hamsters, gerbils, mice, or rats, some owners like to use a soft slicker brush or even a toothbrush to keep them looking sleek.

and constipation. By palpating the pet's abdomen, a veterinarian can feel the stomach and intestines and detect whether the animal has a hairball. However, in other cases an x-ray might be needed. Proper diet and preventive care, along with new medicines, make hairballs easier to manage today.

Ferrets and rabbits are notorious for eating unhealthy

items when they exercise unsupervised in the house. Ferrets are fond of plastic items, and rabbits chew and eat carpet fibers, electrical cords, and other material. These items can also cause digestive blockage and must be diagnosed by a veterinarian. To prevent such occurrences, pet owners must supervise their loose pets.

Depending on the species, surgery is sometimes necessary. Some veterinarians recommend that cat hairball medicine be given to ferrets and rabbits prophylactically. For rabbits, the addition of loose hay, which is high in fiber, can help prevent hairballs and other intestinal problems. Pineapple juice has also been cited as a possible treatment, although it is generally thought to be harmless but ineffective.

Improper Husbandry

An abundance of books and magazines provide information on how to care for small mammal pets properly. When well cared for, pets are

Keeping cages clean is one of the most important ways small animal owners can help their pets stay healthy.

Swollen feet or toes are often the result of unsanitary conditions or keeping the animal on an irritating surface, such as wire flooring with holes that are too wide.

housing or keeping the animal on an irritating substrate.

Small animals often seem to tolerate a dirty environment. This trait is beneficial, because they are frequently children's pets and often suffer from occasional neglect. Small animals are hardy creatures, but their tolerance can eventually diminish and they will become ill if kept in an unsanitary environment.

Few pet owners enjoy cleaning their pet's home. Some animals, such as rabbits, guinea pigs, mice, and ferrets, might need to have the bedding in their cages or litter boxes changed every few days. If you are somewhat lazy, then select a bedding designed to reduce the formation of ammonia from urine so that your pet can better tolerate the interval between cage cleanings. Even with these more sophisticated beddings, you must still prevent the accumulation of feces and urine in your pet's cage.

less stressed and have better natural resistance to diseases. A plethora of problems caused by poor husbandry can affect small pets. "Husbandry" is a big word for the way in which a pet is taken care of, including aspects such as housing, food, and water. A pet is completely dependent upon his owner to provide him with the proper environment. The animal cannot modify the size, temperature, air circulation, or cleanliness of his home. You must place your pet's cage out of the view of other pets and away from direct sunlight, drafts, and excessive temperature and humidity changes.

Clean cages are one of the most important ways small animal owners can help their pets stay healthy. Spoiled food and a dirty cage are invitations to illness. A clean, well-ventilated cage is essential, because the ammonia vapors from urine can irritate an animal's

respiratory tract and allow diseases to develop or aggravate an existing illness. The ailments from improper husbandry can be caused by many things and are usually preventable. Problems with small animals' feet (e.g., swollen feet or toes) are often the result of improper

Ferrets and rabbits can be litter-trained, making cleaning chores a bit easier.

Many ferret owners bathe their pets regularly, although *most* ferrets don't enjoy it! It's important to remember that human soap and shampoo may dry the skin of small pets.

Instead of feeling overwhelmed by the daunting task of a thorough cleaning, and thus postponing it, try using a kitty litter scoop to quickly remove and replace some of the soiled bedding. Doing so can allow the cage to remain sanitary a few extra days before you undertake a more meticulous cleaning. Routine hygiene is the most effective way to prevent disease organisms from becoming established in a pet's home and overpowering a pet's natural resistance to disease. Your pet is most likely to get sick when you become forgetful about cleaning his cage.

Other steps to make cage cleaning easier include buying larger quantities of bedding so you always have some around for a quick change. Most pet care books on small mammals recommend washing food bowls and changing water bottles every day. However well intentioned they may be, many pet owners do not find this practical. Another option

is to have a second set of bowls and bottles that can be quickly filled and used until you have time to wash the first set.

Bathing—Owners of small mammals sometimes wonder whether they should bathe their pets. If an animal is dirty and smelly, it is usually because he has been lying on dirty bedding. Cleaning his cage, providing fresh, sweet-smelling bedding, and allowing the animal to groom himself is usually better than a bath.

Nonetheless, people who exhibit small animals do occasionally bathe them with lukewarm water and a mild shampoo. Immediately drying them with a towel is safest. Hair dryers are not recommended because they can burn the animals' sensitive skin if used improperly.

Because of their pets' natural musty smell, ferret owners bathe their pets with ferret shampoo. However, most ferrets do not like to be bathed. Ferrets should be washed no more than once a week. Excessive bathing can cause problems such as dry, itchy skin.

Neglect—One veterinary reference manual, which describes common clinical conditions affecting small animals, lists starvation and/ or dehydration as a possible cause of sudden death in

Because starvation and neglect is a major cause of death in small pets, it is vital that parents supervise the care of their children's pets.

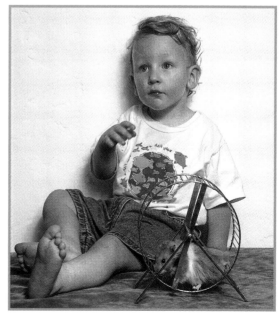

mice, hamsters, gerbils, and rats. It is possible to draw several conclusions from this statement, because such a potential diagnosis is not listed for larger pets such as ferrets, chinchillas, rabbits, and guinea pigs. For example, it is harder for a family or pet owner to ignore the care of a larger animal. Small pets are more easily overlooked. Cases of neglect are often related to children, rather than adults, being the primary caretaker for a pet. Therefore, it is imperative that parents participate in the care of their child's pet, and depending on their child's age, supervise to ensure the safety and health of the pet.

Nails—The nails of small fuzzy animals grow continuously. In some environments, the nails grow faster than they are naturally worn down. Many pet owners complain that long, sharp nails can make handling their pets unpleasant at times. Besides

Trimming a pet's nails can be difficult for a beginner. Have an expert show you how, and then make sure to trim the pet's nails only when he is sleepy.

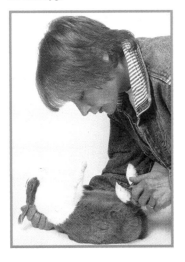

The Sprague-Dawley rat was developed for scientific research and is now found in pet stores everywhere, where it is known by its common name—the hooded rat.

being sharp on human skin, long nails present a hazard to a pet that is allowed to roam loose in the house. Long nails can get caught in carpeting, and an animal's unnoticed struggles can cause the nail to rip or tear out by the root. Clipping the nails on a regular basis will not only help reduce the likelihood of getting scratched, it will also protect the pet from mishaps. Because trimming a small pet's nails can sometimes be difficult (and if done improperly, painful and traumatic) it is often best to have a veterinarian show you how.

However, some pet owners want to do the job themselves. Buy clippers designed for birds or cats (human nail clippers are also OK) and some type of styptic powder to stop any bleeding. The best time to trim the animal's nails is when he is tired, not when he is wide awake and playful.

Using two people is usually best—one to hold the pet and one to clip the nails. Keep the wound powder and some damp cotton swabs handy.

Before attempting to cut your pet's nails, be certain that you know where the quick (the living portion of the nail that contains nerves and blood vessels) begins and ends. If you are uncertain, ask a pet store employee or veterinarian to show you the difference between the quick and the dead portion of the nail. This can sometimes be hard to detect in animals with dark-colored nails, but if you look underneath the nail, you can usually see where the quick ends. The nail should be cut below the quick. If the nail is trimmed too short, it can cause painful bleeding, and your pet might bite if he is in pain. A small cut is usually adequate, just enough to remove the sharp, pointed tip.

Heredity

An animal's heredity (the genetic transmission of traits from parents to offspring) can affect its health. For example, if one parent had a genetic malocclusion, chances are good that some of the offspring might be similarly affected. An animal's genetic susceptibility to various ailments can also vary by breed and strain. For example, certain breeds of rabbit (e.g., Dutch) have a hereditary predisposition for pregnancy toxemia (a condition that occasionally causes the mother rabbit's death late in pregnancy).

Scientists have developed specialized strains of laboratory animals to help them study diseases that affect people and animals. For example, using traditional breeding techniques and newer genetic tricks, scientists have created more than 2,400 strains of mice, each exhibiting some trait that mimics human conditions, including obesity, cancer, Alzheimer's disease, and epilepsy. Although these more recent specialized strains are highly unlikely to be found in the pet trade, previous strains of laboratory animals are available as pets. However, this is not as ominous as it sounds. For example, the Sprague-Dawley rat is the familiar hooded rat available in pet stores. It was developed originally for scientific research and is known to be less susceptible to various conditions than, for example, the albino rat. It is both hardy and good-natured.

While an animal's breed may be obvious, unless you are a serious breeder, it is highly unlikely that you know your pet's strain, nor is such information useful to a pet owner. However, a well-informed veterinarian will be aware of the potential effects of breed and strain on the health of small mammal pets.

Nutrition and Aging

Many diseases are the result of poor or inadequate diet, such as a rodent selectively eating one ingredient, such as sunflower seeds, from a mix. In addition, children often feed their pets inappropriate foods like cookies and potato chips. To prevent diet-related problems, consider feeding nutritionally balanced pellets and treats manufactured specifically for your kind of small animal. Commercial foods should be fresh and sweet-smelling, not rancid or dusty. Store foods in a cool, dark cupboard. Do not expose the food to temperature fluctuations or direct sunlight.

Minimize the potential for obesity by feeding appropriate

Many pet owners feed their pets human junk foods, like sweetened cereals or salty chips. A poor diet can cause disease.

Always feed your pets appropriate foods in the appropriate quantity, and make sure they get plenty of exercise so they will live to a ripe old age.

amounts of food and providing cage accessories that allow play and exploration, such as exercise wheels, tunnels, and ramps. Of course, fresh, clean water is also essential.

Old Age—As your pet gets older, you might begin to notice changes in his behavior and body condition because of aging. Symptoms often appear gradually in old animals, so that pet owners sometimes do not notice. However, middle-aged to older animals are more prone to illnesses than when they were young. Noninfectious ailments such as tumors are usually seen in older animals. Your veterinarian might suggest changes to your pet's diet based on his health. For example, animals with kidney disease should be fed a diet with a reduced amount of protein to reduce the workload on the kidneys.

Deciding whether to euthanize an old pet is very painful. Your veterinarian can help you with this decision. The time to discuss this option is when your pet might not be able to leave his nest, must be force-fed, or is terminally ill. In some cases, it might be better for a pet to be painlessly put to sleep rather than be subjected to treatment such as chemotherapy for a condition that has a poor prognosis.

PREVENTION

Prevention of ailments is far more successful than treatment. Prevention of disease is based on commonsense husbandry practices. Pay attention to your pet's physical health and behavior.

Note any weight changes, check teeth alignment, and feel for lumps and bumps. Significant changes in the amount of food or water consumed and in activity and behavior are also important to note and could signal illness. Knowing your pet's regular behavior is helpful in detecting when he is not feeling well. Prevention also means feeding animals a nutritionally balanced diet, housing them correctly, and practicing good hygiene, such as cleaning the inside of water bottles instead of just refilling them.

Selecting a healthy, genetically sound animal will help to minimize health problems. Carefully check any new pet you are interested in and never bring home an animal with obvious symptoms of illness, no matter how cute he is. A pet's temperament or personality is also important. For a more enjoyable pet-owning experience, choose a friendly animal. Avoid animals that bite, scratch, or run away from your hands. A pet that is tame and friendly will not only make a better pet, he will also be easier for a veterinarian to examine and handle.

THE SICK PET

Taking proper care of a sick pet can help his recovery. Keep the pet in a warm, quiet area and monitor his water and food intake and urine and fecal output. Isolating the animal makes this much easier. A pet with an infectious disease, as diagnosed by your veterinarian, should be isolated from any other small fuzzy pets to prevent the disease from spreading. Infectious diseases can be spread in a variety of ways, including via clothes, hands, and accessories such as food bowls. Be sure to wash your hands and do not share supplies and accessories among an infected animal and other pets without first thoroughly disinfecting each item. Professional breeders are extra cautious and often use disposable surgical gloves when tending to sick animals. Pet owners should handle and feed sick animals last, then wash their hands carefully.

Lethargy and refusal to eat or drink are common signs of illness. Even if your pet lives in an outdoor hutch like this rabbit, make sure to pay close attention to his normal behavior so you can quickly recognize disease symptoms.

Individuals who breed small mammals usually quarantine a new arrival from their other animals, even if the newcomer seems healthy. A new arrival should be kept in a cage as far away as possible from the other animals. The quarantine period should last from two weeks to one month. During this time, the animal's health should be monitored. When the isolation period is over, the newcomer can be moved into the main area. A quarantine period can prevent the transmission of an illness among animals and is highly recommended. Many pet owners routinely acquire additional animals of the same species and do not

Isolate a sick pet in a warm, quiet area and monitor his water and food intake. This will prevent other pets from getting sick and will aid in his recovery.

quarantine the new pets. However, the potential loss of well-loved pets if an outbreak of illness occurs is reason enough to do so.

After any kind of surgery, make sure a pet's cage remains clean to prevent any secondary bacterial infections at the surgery site. Check the incision site each day for swelling or discharge. Be sure to consult with your veterinarian if your pet has not eaten or drunk within 24 hours after returning home, or if there is no urination or defecation.

ZOONOTIC DISEASES

Zoonotic diseases are diseases that can be transmitted from animals to people. It is possible for people to contract a variety of ailments from small mammal pets, but it is not a frequent occurrence. Your veterinarian should be aware of zoonotic diseases such as salmonella and ringworm and can help you take preventive measures if your pet is diagnosed with such an illness.

It is also possible for people or other pet species to make their pets sick. An interesting example is the ferret, which is susceptible to the human flu. The flu virus can be passed from people to ferrets and vice versa. This illness is discussed further in the section on ferrets. Guinea pigs are susceptible to *Bordatella*

infection, the bacteria involved in canine kennel cough complex.

The potential for disease transmission is reduced with proper hygiene, such as washing your hands after playing with pets and cleaning their cages. Purchasing pets from a clean environment rather than a smelly, dirty one also reduces the chance of a small pet having a zoonotic disease.

Although it is not a zoonotic disease, some people have an allergy to small mammals. The allergy can be to the pet's dander, hair, and/or nail scratches. If you develop symptoms such as a rash and sneezing, see your physician for further advice.

Zoonotic diseases are not common, but they do exist. Salmonella, ringworm, the human flu, and kennel cough are just some of the diseases that are contagious to humans or to multiple other species.

SPECIES GUIDE TO COMMON AILMENTS

The following discussion highlights some of the more common or noteworthy ailments that a given species might contract. It is by no means comprehensive, nor does it mean that your pet is likely to become afflicted with any of the illnesses described.

CHINCHILLAS
Common Ailments

Chinchillas tend to have health problems with their digestive systems. They are sensitive to sudden food changes and the addition of fresh greens and fruits to their diet. Because of this

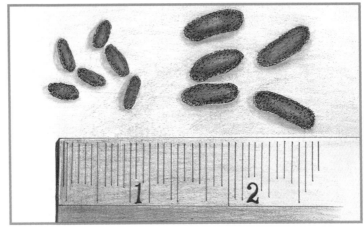

A healthy chinchilla produces plentiful, odorless droppings that are black or brown and shaped like large grains of rice (right). The droppings of a dehydrated or constipated chinchilla (left) will be smaller and drier.

potential, it is important for pet owners to know what normal chinchilla droppings look like so they are more likely to recognize feces that might indicate a digestive problem. A healthy chinchilla produces plentiful, odorless droppings that are black or brown and are shaped like large grains of rice.

Pet owners can minimize the potential risks of digestive problems by feeding their chinchillas pellets made specifically for chinchillas and offering fresh, sweet-smelling hay. Pellets made for chinchillas are long and

Left: Chinchillas are sensitive to sudden food changes and the addition of fresh greens and fruits to their diet. They tend to have digestive problems because of this.

skinny, because they show a preference for this shape as opposed to the fatter pellets made for rabbits and guinea pigs. Sick chinchillas often show the common symptoms of lack of appetite and lethargy. Because such signs are associated with infectious and metabolic diseases, a complete examination by a veterinarian and blood test is needed.

Bloat

Symptoms of a chinchilla with bloat, or gastrointestinal inflammation, include a swollen belly, lying on his side, reluctance to move, and labored breathing. The chinchilla must be treated by a veterinarian, who will decompress the stomach by either passing a gastric tube

Sick chinchillas often show the common symptoms of lack of appetite and lethargy.

When a chinchilla has acute diarrhea, a veterinarian should treat him.

into the stomach or by inserting a needle into the abdomen.

Constipation

Chinchillas are susceptible to constipation, which is thought to be a more common problem than diarrhea. A variety of factors might cause constipation. A frequent cause is feeding a concentrated diet that is high in energy and protein but does not include enough fiber. Increasing the amount of dietary fiber by offering small amounts of fresh fruits and vegetables (e.g., apples, carrots) often solves the problem. Do not feed treats such as grains and raisins, which can aggravate constipation. If the chinchilla does not improve, he should be taken to a veterinarian. The veterinarian might recommend a laxative, such as one made for cats, but will also check for other causes, such as obesity, lack of exercise, intestinal

obstruction, and, if the chinchilla is pregnant, intestinal compression caused by large babies.

Diarrhea

Feeding the wrong foods, such as damp, moldy hay or too much fresh green food, can cause diarrhea. Stress and sudden changes of food can also predispose chinchillas to diarrhea. Besides an obvious lack of solid droppings, pet owners might notice feces matted around their pet's rear end or smeared on the resting board in the cage. Sometimes a chinchilla will recover without treatment. However, in cases of acute diarrhea, a veterinarian might need to rehydrate the animal.

Besides diet, bacterial and parasitic infections can also cause diarrhea. If a chinchilla is also lethargic with dry, dull fur, he should be evaluated by a veterinarian, especially if symptoms are present for more than a few days. Breeding females and young chinchillas up to four months old are most susceptible to infectious diarrhea.

Occasionally, rectal prolapse occurs in chinchillas with severe constipation or diarrhea. The pink rectum can be seen protruding from the chinchilla's anus. This condition must be quickly treated by a veterinarian, who will suture the rectum back in place.

FERRETS
Preventive Care

Ferrets are the only small mammal pet that must receive annual preventive care. A ferret's annual exam is necessary for its yearly rabies vaccine and distemper booster, but the exam is also invaluable for other reasons. A veterinarian will listen to the ferret's heart and lungs, palpate his abdomen, and assess his weight. (Ferrets typically lose weight in spring and gain it back in fall in response to long or short hours of daylight.) This examination can help catch an illness before it is too advanced. Most veterinarians recommend a full blood workup for a ferret that is between three and four years of age. The blood panel can be used to establish a baseline of what is normal for your healthy ferret.

Because ferrets older than three years of age are faced with an increasing probability of disease, many veterinarians recommend health checkups for these ferrets every six months. This will allow a veterinarian to detect potential problems such as enlarged lymph nodes, heart murmurs, skin tumors, and abdominal masses. At five years of age, ferrets are considered geriatric, and a checkup every six months is essential.

Keep in mind throughout your ferret's life that ferrets are true carnivores. Excess fiber or roughage in their diets is very detrimental. The proper diet can help prevent many common gastric ailments in ferrets.

A ferret needs yearly vaccinations. The annual veterinary examination can also detect an illness before it is too advanced.

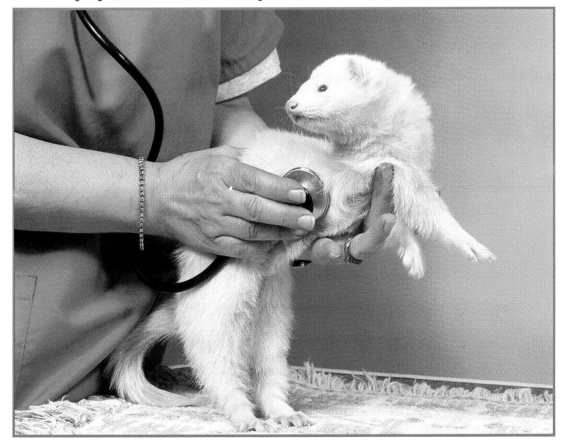

Canine Distemper

Ferrets are susceptible to canine distemper, which is usually fatal sooner or later. The symptoms of distemper in ferrets are similar to a cold, with discharge and crust around the eyes and nose. Ferrets must be vaccinated against this disease. Pet stores and breeders should sell ferrets that have received at least an initial distemper vaccination. After purchase, a veterinarian will need to give your pet additional vaccinations.

These are required at two- to three-week intervals until the series is complete. Thereafter, booster shots are required annually. Only vaccinations labeled for use in ferrets should be used. Dog vaccines may actually *cause* the disease in ferrets.

Insulinoma

Insulinoma is a tumor of the pancreas that causes the pancreas to produce too much

Annual canine distemper booster shots are important for pet ferrets. Only vaccinations labeled for use in ferrets should be used.

insulin, resulting in low blood sugar. This condition is also known as hypoglycemia. If left untreated, insulinoma will cause other important organs to function improperly, eventually causing death. It

occurs most commonly in ferrets between four and five years of age, although it has been documented in ferrets from three to eight years of age.

The onset can be acute or gradual, with symptoms developing over many weeks and months. Sometimes the symptoms are dramatic, such as when a ferret collapses and is mostly unresponsive. Other times, the ferret appears lethargic and weak, with a normal or decreased appetite. An episode can last from several minutes to several hours, during which a ferret has glazed eyes, exhibits excess salivation, and might paw at his mouth. The ferret will either spontaneously recover or he will recover after being given a sugar solution to drink. These episodes are intermittent, with normal activity between periods of weakness.

If diagnosed early, the disease can be managed with diet and medication for up to 18 months. Ferrets with insulinomas must be fed frequently, must avoid prolonged periods without food, and must not eat foods high in sugar or carbo-hydrates. This treatment does not stop the progression of the insulinoma, and gradually increasing doses of medication are usually needed. Surgery is eventually necessary. Although it does not cure the disease, surgery might stop or slow the spread of the insulinoma.

Adrenal Gland Disease

Adrenal gland disease is a common ailment in ferrets. One or both of the adrenal glands, which are located

Ferrets are true carnivores, and excess fiber or roughage in their diets—even a daily cereal hijacking at breakfast—can be detrimental to their health.

above the kidneys, become enlarged and produce excess amounts of hormones. The most common symptom in ferrets with this disease is progressive hair loss, which usually begins on the rump and tail and spreads to the ferret's sides, back, and belly. Often, the hair simply falls out when the ferret is stroked. Other symptoms are also present. Pet owners often bring their female ferrets to the vet because they notice an enlarged vulva. Male ferrets may have difficulty urinating and can develop partial or complete urinary blockage.

No single test is used to diagnose adrenal gland disease. An abdominal sonogram can help to detect an enlarged adrenal gland, and a blood panel that measures hormones produced by the glands can also be used to help diagnose this illness. A veterinarian will

The symptoms of insulinoma in ferrets can be dramatic—a complete collapse—or subtle. Lethargy, weakness, and a decreased appetite are some of the signs.

also inquire about the ferret's general health and activity level. As the disease progresses, veterinarians typically document the areas of hair loss for comparison.

This disease can be treated medically or surgically. However, thus far, treatment with medication does not cure the disease. As scientists and veterinarians learn more about this condition, more effective medical methods of treating it will probably be developed. In the meantime, surgical removal of the diseased adrenal gland is

This ferret's adrenal gland disease has caused the progressive hair loss seen on his back and tail. Both surgical and medical treatment is available for this common ailment.

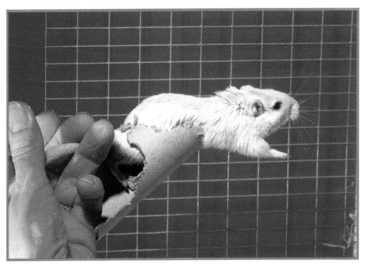

Gerbils are particularly susceptible to fractured bones, bone development problems, and growth problems brought about by inadequate nutrition.

eventually necessary and is usually successful. Following removal, the clinical signs, such as difficulty in urinating, get better, and the ferret will even regrow his hair. Veterinarians prefer to operate on ferrets early in the course of the disease, because a ferret that is weak and sick is less able to withstand surgery.

Adrenal gland disease rarely reoccurs because of metastasis (spread of disease to other parts of the body), although the other adrenal gland might become affected and must then be surgically removed.

Influenza

Ferrets are susceptible to several strains of the human flu. With watery, red eyes, nasal discharge, sneezing, and coughing, infected ferrets look similar to people when they have a cold. It will take about a week for a ferret to recover his energy and appetite and feel well again. Transmission can occur from person to ferret,

through contact with other sick ferrets, and from bedding and accessories. The disease can be serious in a very young or old ferret if secondary bacterial infections develop.

Ferrets are susceptible to several strains of the human influenza virus. If you have the flu, it's best to have another member of the family care for your pets for a few days.

A ferret with signs of a cold or flu might need veterinary treatment.

For prevention, ferret owners should have another member of their household care for their pet when they are sick, or they should wash their hands before and after handling their pet and wear a face mask. There is no treatment to help ferrets recover sooner, and most ferrets become well on their own.

GERBILS
Traumatic Injuries

Gerbils do not appear to be prone to as many potential ailments as many other small mammal pets. Some of the problems they are susceptible to can be prevented with good husbandry. Gerbils are susceptible to fractured bones, bone development problems, and growth problems. It is thought that these ailments are due to inadequate nutrition, because gerbils tend to selectively eat only sunflower seeds from seed-based mixes. Proper nutrition is often best supplied with pellets, since no one ingredient can be picked out.

Skin and Fur

Gerbils often have skin problems. Hair loss and moist skin on the muzzle and nose of gerbils is often due to infection from bacteria and can be "staph" dermatitis. Muzzle dermatitis is another condition that looks similar to staph dermatitis. The loss of hair from the gerbil's muzzle can also be caused by mange mites or self-inflicted trauma. The latter occurs when the gerbil constantly rubs his

Proper nutrition for gerbils can be difficult to achieve, because they tend to selectively eat only their favorite ingredients out of seed mixes. Feeding them pellets may be a good idea if this is a problem.

snout on feeders or the cage itself. Do not use coarse material, such as cat litter or corncob, for bedding. Gerbils like to dig and burrow through the cage substrate, and these materials can cause abrasions on their face. A soft bedding like aspen shavings will work better.

GUINEA PIGS
Common Ailments

Although they are hardy · pets that are easy to care for, guinea pigs are not tough when it comes to visiting the veterinarian. They scream and squeal no matter what the procedure. However, sick guinea pigs lose condition very rapidly. Waiting too long to take a guinea pig to the veterinarian can have fatal consequences.

Scurvy

Like people, guinea pigs cannot make their own vitamin C and must receive sufficient amounts in their diet. Pellets made for guinea pigs are supplemented with vitamin C. However, if the pellets are not fresh enough, the vitamin C can degrade, so the dietary intake will be inadequate.

Guinea pig food bought in grocery stores and drugstores might have a low turnover and is less likely to be fresh. Within two weeks, clinical symptoms can develop in guinea pigs fed food *without* vitamin C. Young, growing guinea pigs are most

Guinea pigs, which are noisy animals by nature, generally scream and squeal during their visits to the veterinarian, no matter how harmless the procedure. However, that is no reason to delay treatment for a sick guinea pig.

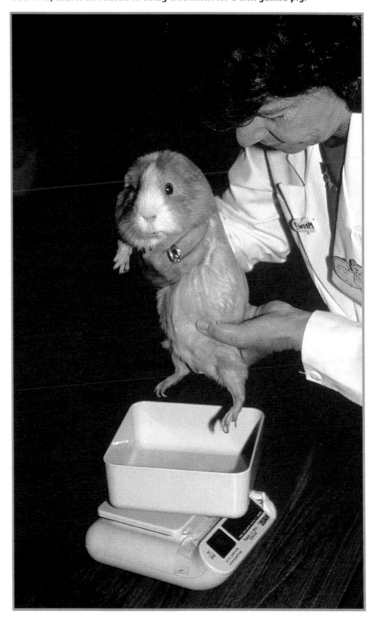

Pelleted food designed especially for guinea pigs will contain extra vitamin C, which is not contained in food made for other animals. This is a vital nutrient for guinea pigs, and deficiencies of it will cause scurvy.

Because a number of different types of bacteria can be involved, a veterinarian must diagnose the type of disease based on clinical signs, such as runny nose, and on the results of a culture to identify the causative bacteria. The infection can become more extensive and spread to the lungs and/or middle ear. Some types of bacteria can enter the blood stream and spread to other parts of the body, such as the reproductive system or joints.

Treatment involves antibiotics and supportive care with injection of fluids to avoid dehydration, supplemental vitamin C, and in some cases, force-feeding. Guinea pigs are considered to be one of the most sensitive to antibiotics of the common small pets. Antibiotics such as tetracyclines and those in

It may be necessary to force-feed guinea pigs with respiratory illnesses. Your veterinarian can show you how to do this safely and easily with a syringe.

susceptible to scurvy. Pregnant and nursing guinea pigs require almost twice as much vitamin C as normal.

Symptoms of scurvy are numerous and include poorly groomed coat, loss of appetite, diarrhea, slow healing of wounds, and a stiff, limp gait. The guinea pig will be in pain and will grind his teeth and even squeal from the pain. Secondary infections and intestinal disorders are more common in guinea pigs with scurvy.

Scurvy can also cause dental problems. Vitamin C is necessary for the formation of collagen, which is found in bones, tendons, cartilage, and connective tissue. Collagen is necessary to keep teeth tightly anchored. Without collagen, the guinea pig's teeth loosen and malocclusion occurs. Feeding fresh pellets should prevent scurvy from developing. In addition, pet stores sell palatable vitamin supplements for guinea pigs.

Respiratory Illness

Guinea pigs are susceptible to respiratory diseases caused by bacteria.

the penicillin family are very dangerous to guinea pigs. Never treat guinea pigs with antibiotics without a veterinarian's expertise.

HAMSTERS
Digestive System
"Wet tail," known scientifically as proliferative ileitis, is a serious intestinal disease of hamsters. A number of bacteria have been implicated as possible sources of the disease. Symptoms are lethargy, lack of appetite, poorly groomed coat, watery diarrhea, and liquid staining around the tail area (thus the name wet tail). Because the diarrhea causes dehydration, affected hamsters need immediate fluid treatment (e.g., electrolyte replacer, such as a diluted sports drink, in the water bottle) and antibiotics. After the first clinical signs appear, affected hamsters that are not treated die in two to seven days. Even with early, aggressive treatment, many hamsters die.

A veterinarian should diagnose and treat the affected hamster. When the cost of a visit to the veterinarian is an impediment, pet stores do sell products that can be used to treat wet tail. However, sometimes this medicine is used too late in the disease process.

Some forms of wet tail are contagious. Any affected hamster should be immediately isolated to prevent the potential spread of this disease. If an outbreak does occur, cages and accessories should be sterilized with a bleach solution. Stress, such as that caused by a new environment, seems to be a precursor of this disease. Wet tail most commonly occurs in weaned hamsters between three and eight weeks old. It is less common in adult hamsters.

Respiratory System
Hamsters are susceptible to respiratory illnesses, but they generally only develop pneumonia if exposed to extreme drafts or dampness. Such conditions should not typically be found in a pet owner's home.

MICE
Skin and Fur
More than other small mammals, mice are susceptible to fur mites. Typical signs are thinning hair, a greasy-looking coat, and excessive scratching. The scratching can lead to scabs, also called self-inflicted ulceration. Areas that are difficult for a mouse to reach

Remedies for wet tail that are sold in pet stores may or may not cure an affected hamster. A veterinarian will be able to accurately diagnose and treat the sick pet.

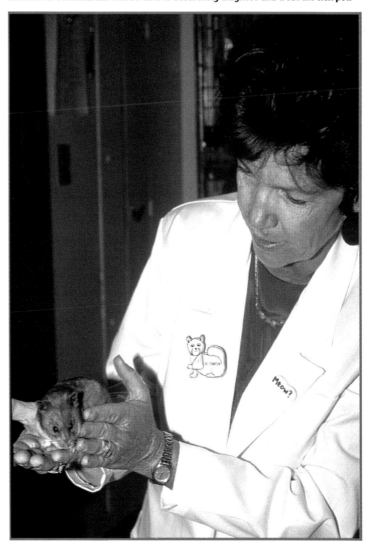

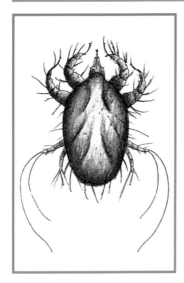

Mice are particularly susceptible to infestation by fur mites similar in appearance to this rabbit mite. Mites cause thinning hair, a greasy-looking coat, and extreme itchiness.

and groom, such as the head and trunk, most often show these symptoms.

Mites are spread by direct contact with infected mice or infested food and bedding. Your mouse might not have been in contact with other animals and other potential sources of infestation such as bedding or food. However, it is possible that the mite infestation was present subclinically for weeks or months before obvious signs developed.

Three types of mites typically affect pet mice. Although wild mice can transmit additional types, few, if any, pet mice come into contact with wild mice. A veterinarian must identify the species of mite by observing the adult mites, nymphs, or eggs on the mouse's hair. Mite infestations are typically treated with ivermectin, which must be provided by a

veterinarian. A veterinarian might suggest that a few drops be placed directly on the mouse's head so that the mouse spreads the medicine through grooming and ingestion. The use of cedar shavings is also known to help repel external parasites.

Lumps and Bumps

Groups of mice sometimes squabble among themselves. Dominant mice might "barber," or cut the hair of, subordinate individuals. Some of these fights get nasty. Mice often gang up on one individual, who may suffer serious wounds. Such lesions often form scabs and heal by themselves. In other cases, a wound becomes infected with bacteria and develops into an abscess. A veterinarian must then treat the abscess.

Few pet mice come into contact with wild mice, so the many kinds of mites that those animals carry rarely affect pets. Pet mice typically contract just three types of mites.

RABBITS
Snuffles

Infection with *Pasteurella* bacteria is the most common infectious disease of rabbits. It can attack any part of a rabbit's body and spread to others. The most common clinical signs are runny eyes, sneezing, and a thick discharge from the nose. In addition, the insides of the rabbit's front legs are dirty from nose wiping. This form of the disease is usually called "snuffles."

Pasteurella is diagnosed from cultures and blood tests. The symptoms are easy to treat, but the disease

Groups of mice may squabble among themselves, causing bite wounds or even "barbering" each other's fur.

Below: Rabbits with the "snuffles," like this unfortunate bunny, have runny eyes, sneezing, and a thick discharge from the nose. Their front paws and the area around their eyes and nose are crusty and dirty from nose wiping.

The most common types of tumors that can be felt under a mouse's skin are mammary tumors and muscle tumors. Tumors of organ systems are unlikely to be detected by pet owners, because such tumors do not necessarily distort the outline of a pet. The incidence of tumors in mice varies according to several factors, including the mouse strain and the presence or absence of mouse mammary tumor viruses. Subcutaneous tumors are almost always malignant. By the time a veterinarian diagnoses the tumor, it has often ulcerated and formed sores. Although the tumor can be surgically removed, the chance of recurrence is high, and likelihood of recovery is not good.

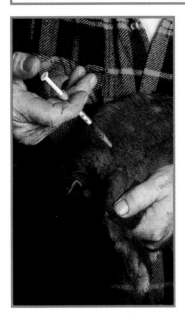

Injected antibiotics are preferred in rabbits, because oral antibiotics can cause additional health problems.

is currently impossible to cure. Antibiotics are used to treat mild cases of snuffles and can relieve an animal's symptoms. Injections are often preferred, because many oral antibiotics cause additional problems.

Since rabbits can die from *Pasteurella*, prevention is best. The disease is easily transmitted by close contact between rabbits. Ideally, new rabbits should be isolated for at least one month. Many rabbits are chronically infected but only show signs of infection when stressed.

Rabbit cages should be clean and odor-free. Ammonia is irritating and can precipitate an outbreak or cause a relapse.

Digestive System

Many diseases of rabbits involve their digestive system. It used to be common for pet owners to feed their rabbits only alfalfa pellets, with occasional treats of lettuce or carrots. Nowadays, pet owners are better informed and know they must offer rabbits older than one year a continuous supply of hay. Pellets should be fed in moderation. Overfeeding pellets can lead to obesity. Obesity causes numerous health problems in addition to complicating surgery if it is ever necessary.

Pet owners sometimes feed their rabbits foods that are inappropriate for rabbits, which are herbivorous animals. Treats that are high in sugar, carbohydrates, protein, and fat, such as breakfast cereals or dry dog food, should not be offered. Besides the fresh vegetables found in your kitchen, pet stores sell appropriate treats for rabbits. However, you

Contrary to popular belief, rabbits cannot live by carrots alone. Pellets should be fed in moderation, and rabbits should have a constant supply of fresh hay to eat. Green foods, such as carrots and lettuce, are a great supplement to this diet.

should only feed treats in moderation. To prevent obesity, reduce the amount of the regular ration by the appropriate amount.

Most rabbit care books now mention cecotropes, so pet owners are more familiar with this phenomena. Cecotropes are small, soft pellets produced by the rabbit's cecum, which is part of his intestinal tract. Cecotropes contain important vitamins and nutrients. They pass from the rabbit's anus and the rabbit eats them immediately. Although this seems repulsive, it is a means by which the rabbit obtains additional nutrients from his food. Overweight rabbits can have difficulty eating their cecotropes, which is an important reason to maintain rabbits at healthy weights. If you observe cecotropes in your rabbit's cage (they look like small clusters of grapes), it usually indicates something is wrong.

Diarrhea often occurs in rabbits. If it is present for more than a few days, the rabbit should be seen by a veterinarian. A variety of possible factors can cause this condition, including coccidia (a one-celled protozoan), which must be diagnosed by a veterinarian. Increasing the fiber in a rabbit's diet by offering only hay is usually part of the treatment.

Traumatic Injuries

Rabbits are prone to broken bones from improper handling. The skeleton of a rabbit is delicate and lightweight compared with its body weight (only seven to eight percent of its body weight), but its muscles, which are developed for running, are extremely strong. Improperly handled rabbits are at risk of fracturing their long leg bones and spines. If they are not securely held when picked up, they can kick violently with their powerful hind legs. Not only can the kicking result in fractures to the leg bones (especially the tibia), the vertebrae can fracture and damage the spinal cord. When pet owners are scratched by the struggling rabbit, they may drop the pet, causing further harm.

Proper handling of a rabbit is essential if injury to the rabbit and pet owner is to be prevented. Never pick one up by the ears or let the rear legs dangle while you carry the rabbit. Grasp the rabbit by the scruff of his neck with one hand and use the other hand to support his hindquarters. When carrying a rabbit, tuck his head under your arm. With his head and eyes covered, the rabbit remains quiet and relaxed. This hold gives you extra security if the rabbit starts to struggle or kick. Be extra cautious when placing the rabbit into his cage or onto the floor. This is the time pet owners are most likely to be scratched, because the rabbit feels least secure.

RATS
Red Tears

Behind the rat's eye lies a pigmented gland called the harderian gland. This gland secretes a red-brown material

Coccidia, a one-celled protozoan, causes digestive problems and is transmitted in contaminated food and water. Proper husbandry will go a long way toward preventing this illness from spreading.

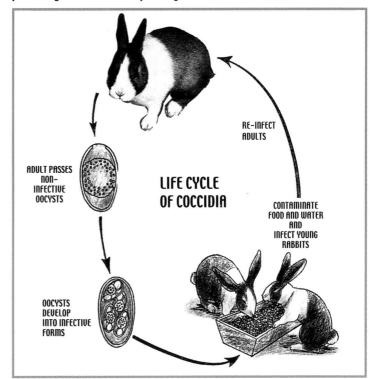

ADULT PASSES non- INFECTIVE OOCYSTS

LIFE CYCLE OF COCCIDIA

RE-INFECT ADULTS

CONTAMINATE FOOD AND WATER AND INFECT YOUNG RABBITS

OOCYSTS DEVELOP INTO INFECTIVE FORMS

Eye secretions in rats are normally colored reddish brown. "Red tears" in rats happens when infection and inflammation in the eye cause too much of the lubricating fluid to be secreted.

(porphyrins) mixed with tears that lubricates the eye and eyelid. Infections, irritation, and inflammation from within the eye can all cause red excretions or a red circle around the eye. You should be alert to the presence of "red tears" as an indication that your pet might be sick and need treatment from a veterinarian.

Respiratory Illness

In rats and mice, the most common respiratory disease is murine respiratory mycoplasma (referred to as MRM). Rats and mice are the principal hosts of the disease-causing bacteria, *Mycoplasma pulmonis*. This disease is highly contagious and incurable. The MRM can be transmitted by direct contact between animals or even when the young are still developing in the mother (called in utero transmission). Antibiotics may alleviate

clinical signs but will not eliminate the infection.

Unfortunately, it is almost impossible for pet stores to avoid selling infected animals, which means that the chances of your pet rat being exposed to the bacteria are high. Try to choose a rat that does not appear to be affected with active symptoms, such as sneezing or wheezing. Of course, if you choose a rat without symptoms from a cage of rats where some animals display symptoms, you will know that your pet has been exposed to the organisms. However, a young rat that exhibits such symptoms is likely to develop more severe, lengthy bouts as he gets older.

The clinical onset is usually slow and progressive. Symptoms such as frequent sneezing gradually get worse over a period of months, but acute episodes can occur in young or very old animals.

The disease can sometimes be subclinical, with signs of infection that are difficult to detect.

There are different strains of *Mycoplasma*, and some strains are more virulent than others. Individual animals also differ in their resistance to the disease. Some exposed animals never display any symptoms. Many pets can live normally when this disease affects their upper respiratory tract. However, if the disease progresses into bronchopulmonary syndrome, the rat can die after several weeks or months. Stress or other bacterial or viral infections can cause an animal to show symptoms suddenly. In most cases, a rat affected with MRM can still live a fairly long life, although it might suffer from occasional severe bouts.

Because viruses and other kinds of bacteria are often involved, MRM is also known as a mixed infection. When this occurs, the animal's symptoms worsen (e.g., rough hair, lethargy, and labored breathing) and spread to involve more than the respiratory system (e.g., the inner ear). The prognosis for survival is then much poorer. A veterinarian can prescribe an antibiotic and/ or a bronchodilator to alleviate severe symptoms and make your rat more comfortable.

Bumps, Lumps, and Mumps

The most common type of tumor occurs in the rat's mammary glands. These tumors can occur in both females and males. The distribution of mammary tissue is extensive, and tumors can occur anywhere from the neck, along the back, to the base of the tail. Mammary tumors can reach such large sizes (up to ten centimeters) that the rat has trouble moving. These tumors must be surgically removed.

The survival following mastectomy is good if the tumor is benign. Recurrence of benign tumors is common, and often, several surgeries will be needed over the life of the pet. (In laboratory settings, rats that have their ovaries removed have a much lower incidence of mammary tumors than those that do not. However, such a procedure is not usually performed on pet rats.) Abscesses are also common lumps that feel like tumors and must be removed.

Rats that look like they have the mumps most likely have a viral infection of the salivary glands. This infection causes the glands in their neck to swell and gives the disease its common name of "mumps." Immediately isolate an infected rat from any other rats you might have, because this disease is highly contagious. Besides swollen glands, an infected rat will initially have inflammation of the nose, and the tear glands can also be affected. Occasionally, the rat's eyes develop lesions. No treatment is available for this disease, The glands will heal in seven to ten days, and within a month, the rat most likely will be well again.

The most common type of tumor in rats is the mammary tumor, as shown here. These tumors can reach such large sizes that they limit the animal's movement.

Skin and Fur

A rat that develops scabs around his face, neck, and shoulders may be suffering from ulcerative dermatitis. This condition can sometimes start when the rat scratches the skin over an inflamed saliva gland. Treatment consists of clipping the toenails on the rat's hindpaws, which are the feet the rat uses to scratch himself, cleaning the ulcerated skin, and applying a topical antibiotic. Ulcerative dermatitis is caused by bacteria. In order to treat this condition successfully, it is imperative that the rat's cage be kept clean to prevent reinfection with the bacteria.

Many mites and other parasites can affect rats—check with your vet if you spot anything wrong with your rat's skin or coat.

This rat is suffering from dermatitis—an itchy skin condition that has caused him to tear out his fur and scratch his back so that scabs have formed. Dermatitis can have many causes, and pet owners should contact a veterinarian if they spot anything wrong with their pet's skin or coat.

BREEDING YOUR SMALL PET

This section is geared toward pet owners who are considering breeding their pets, not someone who is interested in large-scale breeding or breeding animals to exhibit in shows. Breeding small mammals can be fun and interesting. It is exciting to see how many babies are in a litter and what color and types of coats they develop. Sometimes pet owners accidentally find themselves with a litter of babies when a female they purchased from a pet store is already pregnant. This can be particularly exciting when a pet owner unexpectedly discovers a nest of pink babies with their pet. Conversely, there are some interesting phenomena that many people might prefer to do without, such as when a mother cannibalizes her young.

In some cases, a mother abandons her offspring. Caring for such babies is a lot of work, and not always successful, depending on how old the offspring are. Species-specific books provide information on how to care for an abandoned litter. One of the more successful methods is to have another female foster the babies. However, this means that you must have another mother with a litter of a similar age and not too many babies herself.

Breeding will temporarily change your relationship with a female pet. You cannot take a pregnant or nursing female out of her cage to play as much. Sometimes, as with chinchillas, it is recommended that she not be handled for several weeks prior to giving birth. In other cases, the mother animal becomes protective and territorial. You should consider these and other factors when deciding whether to breed your pet. In some cases, breeding a female puts her at risk for life-threatening disease if

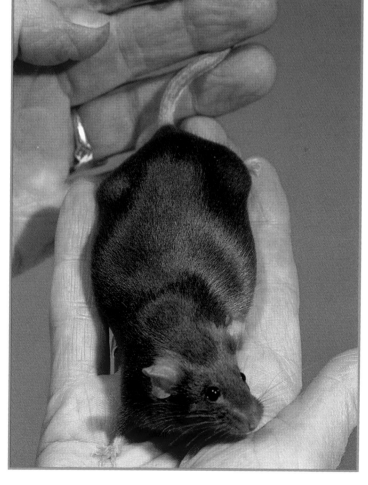

Left: Sometimes, pet owners are surprised to find that the pet they recently purchased is already pregnant, like this dark chocolate mouse.

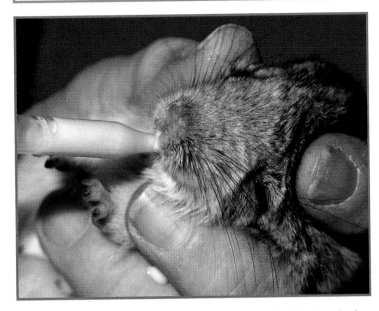

Caring for an abandoned baby animal like this chinchilla is hard work and not always successful. Finding another mother animal to foster the babies gives them a better chance at survival.

consideration of whether or not to breed your pet. Sometimes you might find that there is little demand for the type of pet you breed. Find out what kind of pets are popular in the area in which you live. Certain types of pets are often more popular in some areas than in others.

Do realize that most rats and mice in pet stores are sold as "feeders"—reptile food. Some pet rat and mouse owners do not like the idea that the offspring of their cherished pets might end up in a snake's belly. If this bothers you, consider breeding more expensive specialty strains that pet stores and other fanciers will enjoy solely as pets. Such strains include fancy colors and coat types such as satin or rex. These animals are more delicate and difficult to breed.

In general, breeding small mammals does not present the same problems regarding overpopulation as breeding

you do not pay studious attention to her well-being. No matter what, animals used for breeding must be healthy and in good condition.

FINDING HOMES

Before you decide to breed your pet, consider where you will find homes for the offspring. Friends, teachers (who can keep them as classroom pets), and pet stores are all possibilities. However, if you want to breed more than one litter of youngsters, you will probably need to establish a business relationship with one or more pet stores in your area. This is because many species of small mammals are prolific and can easily produce dozens of offspring in one year.

If you establish a business relationship with a pet store, be sure to keep them apprised of when you will

have babies available. That way, they will not order from their wholesaler or buy other people's pets, and you will be sure to have a place for your pet's offspring.

The demand for the type of animals you want to breed should factor into the

Before you breed your pet, it's very important to find potential homes for the offspring. Teachers who want a pet for their classrooms are one possible source.

Ferret and rabbit owners should think very seriously before breeding their pets, because a large number of these pets are abandoned at animal shelters each year.

dogs and cats does. However, this is untrue of rabbits and ferrets. For various reasons, many pet owners relinquish these animals to rescue groups and animal shelters. Some fanciers and hobbyists involved with these species strongly recommend that all rabbits and ferrets be spayed or neutered to avoid overpopulation.

Usually, the best time for the babies to go to their new homes is shortly after they are weaned. The babies are cutest then and easiest to tame and handle. Their new owners are more likely to enjoy them compared with an older animal that is potentially more difficult to tame. In addition, most books on the

care of small mammals recommend that pet owners buy young animals.

Compared to many livestock wholesalers who distribute hundreds of small mammals, hobbyist breeders have an advantage: they are more likely to produce interesting breeds and varieties with different colors, coats, and textures. Even more importantly, hobbyists are likely to have handled and played with the baby animals so that they will already be used to people. Playing with baby animals and getting them used to interacting with people is fun. Tell the pet store personnel if your stock is already hand-tamed—in some instances, the pet store

might be willing to pay you more.

Although in most cases you will be able to sell your pet's offspring to a pet store, you will not make a lot of money. Commercial breeders efficiently produce multitudes of babies to turn a profit. Most likely, you will make enough money to buy some food and other supplies, but you will probably not make enough money to cover the extra costs of food and supplies incurred by breeding your pets. One exception is chinchillas, which can sell for a high price. However, chinchillas are not always easy to breed and have a gestation period of more than three months.

than usual. In most cases, the female will need a nest box. Pet stores sell wooden nest boxes with lids that lift up for easy viewing. Other alternatives include cardboard boxes or nests that the mother will construct of paper you provide such as unscented tissue or paper towels.

Additional cages and supplies like bowls and water bottles might be necessary if you are not able to find homes for the youngsters right away. In many cases, you might need two cages, one for females and one for males. Many young animals, such as hamsters, can become pregnant shortly after being weaned, when they are between 35 and 42 days old.

Caring for more animals means more work. Cages will need to be cleaned more often so they stay sanitary. More animals means more food will be needed.

The best time for baby animals to go to their new homes is shortly after they are weaned. The babies are cutest then and easiest to tame and handle.

SUPPLIES

Breeding small mammals necessitates obtaining additional supplies. Although some types of small mammals such as gerbils can be permanently housed together, other types such as hamsters need separate cages. Even if a male and female can be kept together, it is prudent to have a separate cage for each animal in case you ever do need to separate them. The breeding female or pair will need a larger cage than if they were not used for breeding.

It is vitally important that a pregnant or nursing mother not run out of water. If necessary, hang an extra water bottle in the cage or provide a larger-sized bottle

You may have a better chance to sell your pets' offspring to a pet store if the babies are already hand-tamed and friendly.

BREEDING AND RAISING YOUNG

Pairing a male and female together is not always that easy. Typically, animals that are paired shortly after weaning have less risk of fighting, although it varies by species (e.g., hamsters are not kept as pairs). No matter what the species, it is usually unwise to put a male and female together without some type of introduction. Otherwise, the likely outcome is a fight, with the female the aggressor and winner. She can often seriously hurt the male. Same-sex animals also often fight. To prevent mishaps, be sure you have accurately determined the gender of your pets before introducing the male and female.

When pairing animals, it is a good idea to put them in two separate wire cages, side by side. Leave them in the cages for three to four days so they can become used to each other. If they want to fight in the early stages of their introduction, they have no opportunity to do so. Use your judgment regarding how close the cages are placed. If the animals are acting aggressive toward each other through the cages, place the cages farther apart.

After a few days, put the female into the male's cage. It is best to pair most small mammals during the day when they are sleepy, rather than at night when they wake up. Never introduce the male into the female's cage, because she might be territorial and attack him. Watch the animals carefully for at least 15 minutes. Although the male might resent the intruder, he is usually accepting when he discovers that the other animal is a female. Typical signs of friendliness are sniffing each other, rubbing noses, smelling, or mutual grooming.

If they have settled down with no signs of fighting, they will most likely pair successfully. If the female immediately attacks the male, separate them. You might need to use gloves or have a towel handy that can be thrown over one of them. If they act frightened, growl, or hiss, also separate them. In the latter case, they should be placed back into adjacent cages and given more time to become acquainted.

A female is receptive to mating with a male when she is in estrus. This condition is also known as "coming into season" or "in heat." Experienced breeders can recognize when a female is in estrus, but it is more difficult for pet owners. Depending on the species, most pet owners keep a male with a female for several days to ensure successful breeding.

Many females reach sexual maturity before they are fully grown. Most experts recommend waiting to breed the female until she has reached her adult size. Many types of rodents can become pregnant again just a few hours after delivering a litter. If you do not want your pet to become pregnant again, be sure the male is out of the cage at this time.

In most cases, the pregnant or nursing mother animal will need a nest box like this one. She will be able to climb out, but the low walls will protect the babies. Many nest boxes have a lid that lifts up for viewing.

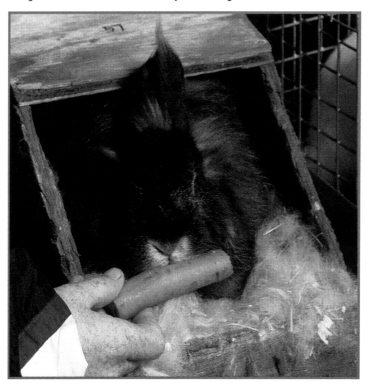

When pairing the male and female animals, place them next to each other in two separate wire cages for a few days so they get used to each other.

Sometimes a female will have a pseudopregnancy, which follows an infertile mating. The female will appear as if she is pregnant, but about halfway through the gestation period, the signs of pregnancy will disappear. The female can then be mated again.

A pregnant female will eat noticeably more food. Once she is nursing her litter, her food intake increases even more. In some cases, the female will need two to three times her normal amount of food. This means that there will be more droppings and urine in the cage. A dirty cage can be an invitation to disease. While the mother will keep the nest area clean, you can often scoop out soiled bedding (away from the nest area) and replace it with clean bedding. The mother animal licks her babies' rear ends to stimulate urination and defecation until they are able to go on their own. (Mothers of precocial young, such as guinea pigs, do not build a nest.)

Most mother animals are easily stressed by changing conditions or environments. Avoid excessive noise, poor lighting, and cold or hot temperatures that create uncomfortable nursing conditions for the female. After her babies are born, keep your disturbance of the mother to a minimum. The nesting material can usually be replaced once the babies are exploring outside the nest.

Once the babies have left the nest and begun to nibble on solid food, provide extra rations so that the animals always have food available. Be sure the water bottle is low enough for the youngsters to drink from it. They will imitate their mother and sample the water from the bottle. While the water bottle must be low enough for the babies, it should not touch the bedding or else the water might leak out of the bottle. Naturally, with more animals eating, the dirtier the cage will become, and the more often it will need to be cleaned.

SPAYING AND NEUTERING

Veterinarians and breeders often recommend spaying or neutering an animal once its breeding life has ended. Doing so can reduce the risks of cancer to the reproductive organs. It can also lessen the likelihood of unacceptable behaviors such as spraying urine.

Most mother animals are easily stressed by disturbances. Avoid changing the cage environment or handling the babies until they are at least several days old.

SPECIES GUIDE TO BREEDING

CHINCHILLAS

Distinguishing the Sexes

The distance between the anus and genital opening for males is approximately twice that of the female. The male has no scrotum, because the testes are in the groin. A female has three pairs of nipples, one set in the lower belly and two pairs below her forearms.

How To

Chinchillas are long-lived animals (up to 20 years) and are able to breed until they are eight years old. They are ready to breed when they are between seven and ten months old. If a male is anxious to breed, he makes a cooing noise. Females that are interested in mating rub their chins on the floor or side of the nesting box, as do the males.

Most pet owners breed chinchillas as pairs. They can be housed together for their entire lives, and most will breed successfully.

Chinchillas can be bred in pairs or in polygamous groups (one male with five to ten females). Because they are expensive, most pet owners breed them as pairs. Introduce the male and female when they are between six and eight months old. Be sure to provide a large enough cage, because they can be housed together for their entire lives. Most pairs get along well and breed successfully. To further reduce the chance of the chinchillas fighting, it is best to pair chinchillas that have just been weaned. It is more difficult to pair adults, which can be unpredictable in their behavior. They should be introduced in wire cages side by side, as described in the introductory breeding section.

The female is receptive to mating for about 4 days and comes into heat every 28 to 35 days. Estrus can be confirmed because the female's vulva is closed except during estrus and birth. Mating can be confirmed by

In chinchillas, the distance between the anus and genital opening for males (left) is approximately twice that of the female (right). The female also has three pairs of nipples, which the male does not.

finding a copulatory plug, also called a "stopper," in the cage. This solid, dime-sized mass falls out of the female's vagina several hours after mating. A breeder can note when the plug is found to determine the female's due date.

Pregnancy and the Young

The gestation period is variable and can range from 111 to 128 days. After about two months, a female will show signs of being pregnant.

Because the gestation period is so long, the easiest way to be certain that a female is pregnant is to weigh her. She should gain about an ounce or more each month. Naturally, you might be able to detect that she is becoming heavier when you pick her up.

In the early stages of pregnancy, a female's teats are often flabby and white in color. After about 60 days, her teats become fuller and reddish in color. If this is her first pregnancy, you should reduce how much you handle her.

As her due date approaches, some breeders add milk powder or calf manna to the female's diet. Be sure that the nest box and cage are clean. Chinchillas do not make a nest, but lining the cage with straw or paper towels will prevent injury and assist drying the young at birth.

Withdraw the dust bath several days before the mother is due to give birth, because the dust can irritate

her genital opening. Do not reintroduce the dust until a week after she has given birth. When the young nurse the first few times, it is best if they do not inhale any dust that remains in their mother's fur.

The male can be removed before or when the young are born. When the parents are kept as a pair, this is usually not necessary, as long as the male does not bother the offspring and the female accepts his presence.

Baby chinchillas are called kits and are precocial—like guinea pigs, they are born fully furred and with a complete set of teeth. They are able to move shortly after being born. They are born extremely wet and could

This baby chinchilla, pictured with his parents, is just one hour old. Chinchillas are born very wet and should not be exposed to cold or drafty conditions at birth.

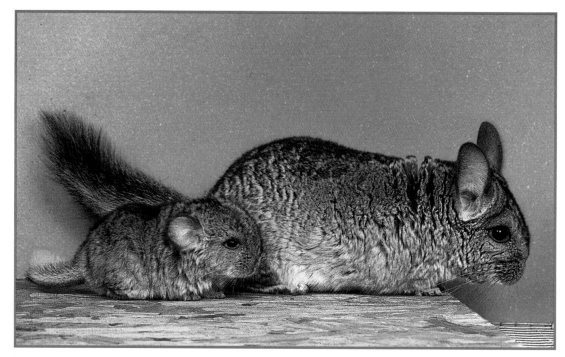

Chinchillas are born precocial—fully furred and able to walk. Despite this, they are not weaned until around seven weeks of age.

succumb in cold conditions, so be sure the mother's cage is not cold or drafty. Within a day of birth, the babies' eyes have opened.

The normal litter size ranges from two to four kits per litter, but as many as eight have been born on rare occasions. It is normal for the mother to lose fur around her nipples as the kits suckle, but the fur will ultimately regrow. Chinchillas nurse their offspring for a comparatively long time. They are usually not weaned until around seven weeks of age. The babies begin to eat solid food at 12 to 14 days. Be sure to separate young chinchillas by the time they are four months old to prevent any accidental breedings.

Potential Problems

Another nursing female will usually accept orphaned newborn chinchillas. Fostering is most likely to be successful if the orphans are close in age to her own offspring. Some breeders have used guinea pigs as foster mothers. In large litters, the babies sometimes fight with each other over access to their mother's teats. In some cases, it may be necessary for a veterinarian to clip their incisor teeth to prevent the babies from injuring each other or the mother's teats.

FERRETS

Serious ferret fanciers and many veterinarians advise against breeding pet ferrets. There are several important reasons for discouraging owners from breeding their pets. Of greatest significance is that breeding ferrets is not as simple as breeding most other small mammal pets.

Breeding requires attentive care and oversight of the mother during gestation, birth, and lactation. Any problems that are not detected and promptly treated can result in the death of the mother ferret. Second, because there are numerous older ferrets in need of homes, rescue clubs do not want to have increasing numbers of abandoned ferrets in need of new homes. Finally, most of the ferrets sold in pet stores are already neutered (males) or spayed (females), so it is not possible to breed them.

Distinguishing the Sexes

Female ferrets are called jills and males are called hobs. Baby ferrets are called kits. Male ferrets can be distinguished from females by the greater distance between the anus and genitals.

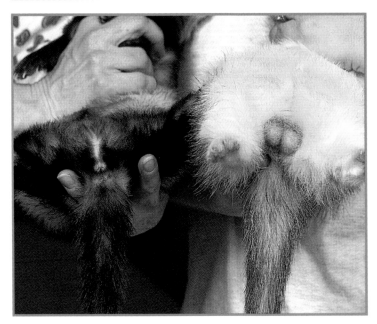

Male ferrets (right) can be distinguished from females (left) by the visible scrotum and the greater distance between their anus and genitals.

How To

The length of daylight affects the reproductive cycle of ferrets. If females are exposed to light for longer than 12 hours a day, they can come into heat for the first time at 4 months of age.

However, the best age to pair females and males is when they are between 8 and 12 months old. A female ferret stays in heat until she has mated. If she does not become pregnant, she will develop a life-threatening disease called aplastic anemia. This condition makes the ferret severely anemic. It is treated by spaying the jill as early as possible if she isn't bred. A swollen vulva is the most common sign of this dangerous condition.

The jill must be provided with a nest box, which can be as simple as a converted litter box. Any soft, washable material or aspen shavings may be used as bedding.

Ferrets are capable of breeding all year long and can get pregnant immediately after giving birth. Females typically have two litters a year.

Pregnancy and the Young

Before breeding, the jill and hob must be fed a diet that contains at least 35 percent protein and 15 percent fat. During pregnancy, the mother ferret must never run out of food. Some breeders offer the mother water in a dish, in addition to her water bottle. The length of the gestation period is 41 to 42 days. First-time mothers have slightly shorter gestation periods. At least a week before the jill is due to deliver, place her cage in a quiet location away from any distractions. In particular, first-time mothers should not be disturbed. An unfamiliar, noisy environment with distractions can cause a jill to reject her litter.

Ferret kits are born hairless, with their eyes and ears closed. These baby ferrets are two days old.

A baby ferret's eyes do not open until he is more than a month old, but he will explore outside the nest and nibble on solid food at three weeks of age.

The jill must be provided with a nest box. She should be able to enter and leave the box easily, but the kits should not be able to climb out. Soft shredded aspen or a small terry cloth can be used for bedding.

Ferrets have relatively large litters. Jills that are well fed and receive appropriate care have between eight and ten kits. It takes the mother about two to three hours to deliver all of her babies. The kits are born hairless, with their eyes and ears closed. For the first two weeks of their life, the kits have little ability to maintain their body temperature. A jill that has bonded with her offspring rarely leaves the nest for the first few days. Make sure food and water dishes are placed close to the nest box so she can remain with her offspring. Except when their mother leaves the nest, the babies lie quietly next to her, nursing and sleeping.

Breeders and veterinarians recommend that the dietary fat level be increased to 30 percent for the first two to three weeks while the mother is lactating.

The kits' eyes open around 30 to 35 days of age. Even before their eyes have opened, the kits begin to explore outside the nest and nibble on food at three weeks of age. The babies are usually weaned when they are six weeks old, although some litters are not weaned until eight weeks of age.

Potential Problems

Numerous things can go awry with a pregnant ferret, which is why breeding ferrets requires constant supervision and oversight of the mother.

A jill in late gestation is susceptible to pregnancy toxemia. This condition is caused by insufficient caloric intake. Missing even one meal is sufficient to

Litters of ferrets are weaned when they are between six and eight weeks old.

cause this ailment. Pregnancy toxemia is a life-threatening condition. A jill that becomes lethargic shortly before her due date could have this disease and must be seen immediately by a veterinarian.

While experienced mothers rarely reject their offspring, new mothers sometimes do. A foster ferret mother must take care of orphaned kits. They are almost impossible to hand-rear and require 24-hour attention. Nursing mother ferrets usually accept orphaned kits of any size or age. However, one must still be careful not to overburden any one mother with too many kits.

Ferrets with small litters (one to two babies) are usually late in delivering their offspring. Consult a vet around the 42nd day of pregnancy. Ultrasonography

and/or x-rays can help your vet decide if a cesarean section must be performed.

Small litters often do not survive, and some jills do not produce sufficient milk.

GERBILS
Distinguishing the Sexes

Gerbils can be sexed when they are about a month old. A male gerbil can be distinguished from the female by the development of a scrotum, which looks like a dark area of skin near the base of the tail. Adult males can be distinguished from females by the greater distance between the anus and the genital opening. In addition, males are slightly heavier than females.

How To

It is best to breed gerbils as monogamous pairs. Buy two

young gerbils and introduce them to each other by the time they are two months old.

Some professional breeders use polygamous harems. They house one male with two to three females. The harem is housed together before the gerbils are eight weeks old. Even so, the gerbils might still fight. It is difficult and usually impossible to pair adult gerbils for breeding. Adults will typically fight and can inflict fatal wounds on one another.

Gerbils will breed all year round. If you are going to keep a mixed pair together, be sure to purchase a cage large enough for a family. The male can typically be kept with the female and pups without any problems.

Pregnancy and the Young

Females can begin breeding when they are between 65 and 85 days old. Males are sexually mature between 70 and 85 days old. Do provide the female with a nest box and nesting material. The gestation period for gerbils varies between 24 and 26 days. Usually, the female will give birth at night. A female can have between three and seven pups, with five being the average. Like many other rodents, the female is immediately able to become pregnant after giving birth. If you do not want her to become pregnant so soon, temporarily place the male in a separate cage.

Young gerbils begin to nibble on solid food at 15 days of age. Be sure to provide soft, small-sized pellets within easy reach of the youngsters. The babies can be weaned between 21 and 24 days of age. By two

A pair of gerbils and their litter will need to have their cage cleaned more often because of the crowded conditions.

months of age, the young gerbils should be separated by gender so no accidental breedings occur.

Potential Problems

Moisture, urine, and feces can build up in an aquarium, especially when the baby gerbils begin to eat solid food. Although a pair of gerbils

might need their cage cleaned once a week, with a litter of babies, plan on cleaning the cage at least every few days.

If the mother gerbil is disturbed, sick, or housed in crowded conditions, she might cannibalize or abandon her litter. In some cases, another mother gerbil will care for the young if she has offspring of a similar age. Females have been known to destroy litters if they stop lactating or if the babies are very small.

GUINEA PIGS
Distinguishing the Sexes

Male guinea pigs are called boars and females are called sows. Boars have obvious scrotal sacs and large testes. The penis can be protruded by placing gentle pressure at its base. Females have a Y-shaped depression above their anus. In addition, females have one pair of nipples in the lower portion of their belly.

How To

Female guinea pigs can become pregnant when they are only six weeks old. Males

Gerbils are born helpless and hairless after 24 to 26 days of pregnancy.

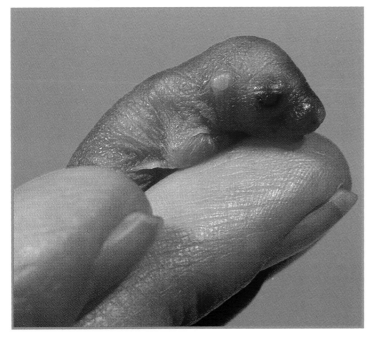

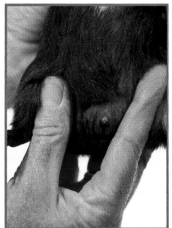
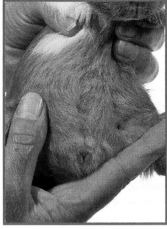

Male guinea pigs (left) are called boars, and the females (right) are called sows. Boars have obvious scrotal sacs and large testes.

Pregnancy and the Young

A guinea pig has a long gestation period—from 59 to 72 days, with 68 days being the average. Several factors can affect the duration of gestation, including litter size and strain. The gestation period is shorter in guinea pigs that have previously borne young and in those with small litters.

After about a month of gestation, it will be readily apparent that a guinea pig is pregnant. A female can double her weight during pregnancy. You must be very careful when handling a pregnant sow. To pick up your pet, carry her upright by holding one hand beneath her rear quarters to support her heavy

reach sexual maturity when they are between nine and ten weeks old. The best age to breed the female is between three and six months.

Guinea pigs can be kept as monogamous pairs, or one boar can be kept with several females. The guinea pigs must be introduced in separate cages, as described

Boars and sows may be kept together or separately. If they are kept separately, they must be introduced slowly. Here, a boar checks out the sows' pen.

in the introduction. If the female(s) do not get along with a male, you should try again with a different partner. Guinea pigs will

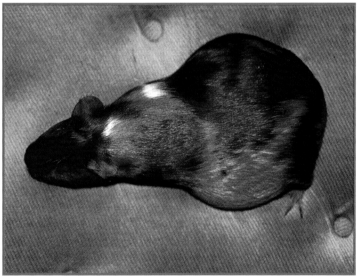

A female guinea pig can double her weight during pregnancy, and her condition is unmistakable after about a month.

breed throughout the year. The female is ready to mate every 14 to 18 days. Until then, the male must keep up a constant courtship. Finding a copulatory plug is one method breeders use to confirm that the guinea pigs have mated.

body. Use your other hand to hold her upper torso beneath her upper arms.

The female does not build a nest, so it can be difficult to determine when birth is near. Because the babies are usually born at night, dusk, or dawn, it is often a surprise

Baby guinea pigs are called pups and are typically weaned after three weeks.

for a pet owner to see the little ones scampering around. Baby guinea pigs are called pups, not the more endearing name of piglets.

A female usually has between two and four offspring. The birth of each pup is rapid, and there are only a few minutes between the births of each baby. The mother licks each baby clean and consumes the afterbirth.

Baby guinea pigs are precocial—they are born fully furred with eyes open and are able to stand shortly after birth. They begin nibbling on solid food at two days of age. The pups are typically nursed for three weeks, after which they are weaned.

The babies are not at risk of being deliberately injured, although adult pigs might sometimes inadvertently trample the young.

Remove the weaned guinea pigs by 21 days so the male does not breed with his offspring.

Potential Problems

Veterinarians highly recommend that female guinea pigs be bred before they are six months old if at all. After six months, the bones of the female's pelvic canal (called the pubic symphysis) fuse and may not adequately separate to allow passage of the baby guinea pigs. The sow can have problems delivering her young, which is a life-threatening emergency. The mother must immediately be taken to a veterinarian who can perform a cesarean section. A female can also have difficulty delivering her babies if she is overweight or her babies are very large.

If possible, orphaned guinea pigs should be fostered by another nursing guinea pig. Lactating sows allow the young of other females to nurse.

It is easier to foster the orphans with another mother rather than caring for them yourself. However, because

baby guinea pigs are precocial and can eat solid food a few days after birth, they are one of the easier orphaned animals to care for. Use evaporated milk diluted with equal parts water. With an eyedropper, feed the babies every two hours until they are five days old. Every four hours after that age is sufficient. At two days of age, offer the babies small amounts of fresh guinea pig pellets moistened with water or formula. Be aware that pups often do not survive if they do not receive sow's milk for the first three to four days of life.

The minimum size of a cage for a breeding female is two feet by two feet. Be certain that the wire mesh is small enough that the babies' feet and legs will not fall through the wire spaces and be injured.

HAMSTERS
Distinguishing the Sexes

The anus and the genital opening of a female hamster are very close, whereas the distance is much farther apart in a male hamster. A female hamster is also slightly larger than a male, with a rounded pelvis. The male's body tapers toward his tail, and the scent glands on his hips are much more obvious.

How To

Hamsters are solitary animals and can be pugnacious with each other.

They can be difficult to pair. Because they fight, they cannot be bred in colonies or in monogamous pairs. Introduce the pair as described in the breeding introduction. The female is usually receptive to a male during early evening. Place the female into the male's cage about one hour before dark. Watch for fighting, and return the female to her cage if she attacks the male. If a male is seriously injured, he might need to be taken to a veterinarian. After they have mated, the male should be returned to his own cage.

A mother hamster needs a cage two to three times larger than a cage for a single hamster. To prevent the baby hamsters from accidentally falling out of a wire cage, be sure the bars are not spaced farther than a quarter-inch apart. Breeding hamsters should be housed in cages with solid floors. Bedding should also be piled completely over the wire floor so no babies fall through to the cage bottom or get stuck. Mother hamsters will use a nest box, either cardboard or wood.

Pregnancy and the Young

In a little less than two weeks, you should be able to tell if the female is pregnant, because she will gain weight and her belly will swell. Following an infertile mating, a pseudopregnancy can last between 7 and 13 days.

Hamsters have the shortest gestation period of any known mammal—only 16 days. At two weeks, clean the female's cage one last time and provide your hamster with a week's supply of fresh food and water. Plan on not disturbing your hamster for about one week after her litter is born.

The average litter size is six, but usually ranges from five to nine. Like rats, mice, and gerbils, baby hamsters are altricial, meaning that they are born pink and naked.

Shortly after birth, guinea pigs are able to stand. They are born with fur and with their eyes open.

By the end of the first week, fur begins to grow.

Their ears open during the second week, when the young leave the nest and begin to nibble solid food. When the baby hamsters are one week old, be sure the water bottle is low enough for the babies to reach.

On the 12th day, the eyes of the baby hamsters open. The young are weaned between 20 and 25 days of age.

Separate the youngsters by gender when they are five weeks old. Female hamsters can become pregnant when they are only 42 days old,

Baby hamsters are extremely small at birth. The bars of their cage should not be more than a quarter-inch apart to prevent them from accidentally falling out.

By the end of the first week of life, a baby hamster's fur begins to grow. The ears and eyes open during the second week.

You should separate the baby hamsters by gender when they are five weeks old, shortly before they reach their sexual maturity.

MICE
Distinguishing the Sexes
As with many rodents, the distance between the anus and genitals is much farther apart in males than in females. In addition, the male's scrotum is usually obvious. Only females have two parallel rows of nipples along their abdomen. They show if you part the hair on the mouse's belly or blow the hair aside. Male mice are called bucks and females are called does.

How To
Females are ready to breed when they are between 50 and 60 days old. Males can breed sooner, at about 50 days old. Mice can be kept in pairs or in colonies of one male to two to three does. Mice come into season every four to five days throughout the year, and immediately after giving birth.

The female is usually receptive to mating in the evening, and estrus lasts for 12 hours. Since the male is kept with the female(s), breeders do not need to keep track of when a female is capable of becoming

and males are sexually mature between 45 and 75 days of age.

Potential Problems
It is best not to disturb the female and her newborn young. When disturbed, some mothers will stuff the babies into their cheek pouches along with food and bedding. The babies can suffocate in her pouches. Other times, the mother might actually cannibalize her offspring or abandon her litter. Unfortunately, both potential situations are common. Because hand-rearing or fostering babies with another mother

hamster is rarely successful, do not disturb the mother for at least one week after birth.

Female mice are ready to breed between 50 and 60 days old, and males can breed at about 50 days. Pictured is a male on the right and a pregnant female on the left.

58

Here, a visibly pregnant female mouse sniffs the newborn litter of a cagemate. The abdomen of a pregnant mouse can grow to enormous proportions.

pregnant. Female mice can breed for seven to nine months, during which they can produce six to ten litters.

Pregnancy and the Young

Some pregnant female mice grow incredibly large, and their lower bellies can swell to three to four times the normal size. The gestation period is usually three weeks. At two weeks, mammary development is noticeable, and the female should not be unnecessarily handled. If the mating was sterile, a female may go through a pseudopregnancy of one to three weeks' duration. When she is close to giving birth, the female prepares a nest. Although mice will make a nest in the cage bedding, they prefer a nest box. Offer the mother unscented tissue or commercial nesting material.

The normal litter size is 10 to 12 babies. A female's first litter is usually smaller than subsequent litters. If the mouse is too young or is over ten weeks of age at first breeding, she may have reduced fertility. Do not disturb the mother for about a week after she has given birth.

Baby mice are born pink and hairless. Their eyes and ears are sealed shut. By the time they are a week old, the babies have a fine covering of fur, and it is even possible to tell what colors they will be.

These baby mice are one week old and they already have a fine covering of fur.

This mother mouse is not only nursing her older litter, but the newborn litter of a cagemate as well. In a breeding colony situation, the young frequently nurse from several mothers.

Their ears and eyes open by the time they are two weeks old. The babies leave the nest and begin to nibble food and explore the cage at about the same time. In a breeding colony situation, several mouse families may occupy a single nest, and the young may nurse from several mothers.

Potential Problems
Mother mice sometimes cannibalize their offspring if they have not been well fed or are exposed to excessive disturbance.

RABBITS
Distinguishing the Sexes
Female rabbits are called does and males are called bucks. Baby rabbits are called kits, bunnies, or kittens. The distance between the anus and the genital opening is greater in the male. The males can also be distinguished from the females by protruding the penis, using gentle pressure

The male rabbit, or buck, has a round genital opening, whereas the female's, or doe's, is a slit, as shown in this illustration.

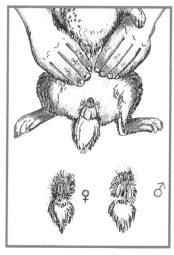

on either side of the genital opening. The male has a round genital opening, whereas the female's is a slit. Unlike most mammals, the male's scrotal sac is above the penis. Does have four to five pairs of nipples, while the male has none. Adult female rabbits have a large fold of skin over their throat that is known as the dewlap.

How To
Female rabbits mature earlier than males. They are ready to breed between four and nine months of age, while male rabbits can breed when they are between six and ten months old. The large variation is due to differences between the various rabbit breeds. The larger breeds take longer to mature than the dwarf and medium-sized breeds.

Does do not have an obvious estrus cycle. They are induced ovulators, which means mating is necessary to stimulate ovulation. Ten hours after mating, the female rabbit ovulates. Although they have no cycle, females are most receptive to a male every four to five days.

Introduce the rabbits as recommended in the introductory section. Always introduce the female rabbit into the male's cage. Males that have been bred before will usually mate with a receptive female within several minutes after the introduction. Inexperienced males take longer.

When uninterested, a female will thwart a male's attempt to mate. She might run away, bite, or vocalize.

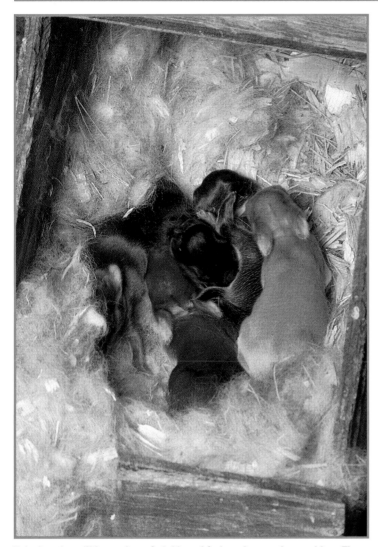

Baby bunnies will be most comfortable and feel most secure in a nest box. The mother rabbit will pull fur from her chest to line the nest.

Provide a pregnant rabbit with a nesting box. Pet stores sell wooden boxes with lids that lift for easy viewing, or you can use a sturdy cardboard box. The nest box should be cozy but also large enough for the female to easily stand up to her full height. A door opening several inches above the cage floor is best. This way, the doe can hop in and out without the babies falling out.

Rabbits usually give birth in the early morning. Does pluck the hair from their chest and dewlap to line their nests several hours to a few days before giving birth. If your rabbit does not do so, offer her unscented tissue or paper towels for nesting material. Within 30 minutes of the first birth, a mother rabbit has usually completed birth of all young.

The litter size of rabbits ranges from four to ten kittens. The kittens are born hairless, blind, and helpless. Mother rabbits nurse their young once a day, for only about five minutes. However, a baby bunny can drink up to 20 percent of its body weight during this brief time. Sometimes, the mother might be slow to start nursing, but within 24 hours the baby rabbits should have received their first meal. Because the mother rabbit stays with the young only briefly while feeding them, pet owners sometimes think the mother is not feeding the babies.

Do not remove the babies if you think the doe is not feeding them. Instead, quickly check the babies. You can tell if the kittens are being fed because their skin will not be wrinkled, and the kittens will

After they have mated, remove the female to her own cage.

Female rabbits can produce offspring for one to three years after maturity, and depending on the breed, bucks can breed for five to six years. Thereafter, many veterinarians recommend that they should be spayed or neutered. Spaying females as early as possible greatly reduces the risk of uterine cancer.

Pregnancy and the Young

The length of the gestation period varies from 29 to 35 days. Larger breeds of rabbit have longer gestation periods. The litter size depends on the breed and whether or not the female has had a litter before. Many of the large breeds tend to produce large litters, whereas the smaller breeds have small litters. First-time mothers usually have smaller litters than in their subsequent pregnancies.

Rabbits are born blind and hairless (above) and begin to grow fur in the first week (below). Their eyes open at ten days of age.

be warm and snuggled together. Professional and serious breeders often weigh the bunnies at the same time each day to assess their growth. The doe will not reject the handled babies. Otherwise, do not disturb the babies until their eyes open, at ten days. On approximately the 12th day, the kittens' ears open. The youngsters are weaned between four and six weeks of age. Then you can start to play with the babies and socialize them to people.

Potential Problems

Pet owners who find themselves with an orphaned litter must work hard to rear the babies successfully. Inexperienced petkeepers sometimes feed the babies too often and too much—they

Below: Mother rabbits nurse their young just once a day. Do not be concerned if it seems that the mother is not feeding her babies unless they appear unhealthy.

Left: When the baby rabbits are weaned between four and six weeks of age, you can start to play with them and socialize them to people.

will descend, and you will be able to see that he is a male.

How To

Rats can be bred in monogamous or polygamous pairs. Pet owners usually breed rats as monogamous pairs. The pair is kept together even when the female has babies. Commercial breeders who need to produce large numbers of rats use the polygamous system. One male is typically housed with two to six females. In some cases, the male is moved among the females' cages. He is always removed before the birth of the young and is reintroduced after a female's

babies are weaned. A mother rat requires a cage several times larger than normal. Not only will she need space, the babies will need space to play once they leave the nest.

Rats can produce young when they are only 50 to 60 days old. However, the best age to begin breeding pet rats is when they are three to four months old.

A female rat's estrus cycle lasts four to five days. The estrus period during which she can get pregnant lasts 12 hours and usually begins in late afternoon or evening. A female rat should get pregnant if the pair are kept together for at least a week.

PREGNANCY AND THE YOUNG

A rat will look pregnant about two weeks after mating.

only need to be fed once a day. The caretaker must stimulate the babies to urinate and defecate after each feeding. Use a cotton ball dipped in warm water to gently wipe their rear ends. When the babies' eyes are open, offer them pellets and hay. When they are ready to be weaned, you will need to add cecotropes from their mother or another adult rabbit so they receive the appropriate bacterial flora.

RATS
Distinguishing the Sexes

Female rats are called does and males are called bucks. Baby rats are referred to as kittens or pups. Generally, in young rats, the distance between the anus and the genital papilla is 50 percent greater in males. A slight swelling is present where the male's scrotum will be. If you hold the rat upright, the testes

In a male rat (left), the scrotum is clearly visible when he is held upright. A female is pictured at right.

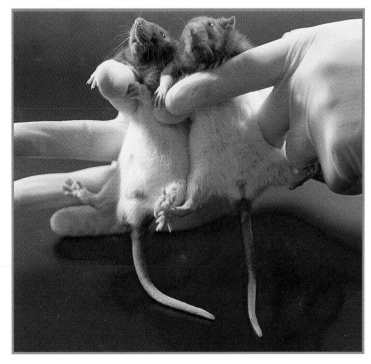

Her lower belly will swell and her appetite will greatly increase. The gestation period is between 21 and 23 days. A female rat may have a reproductive breeding life of 9 to 16 months. During this time, she can bear seven to ten litters. Within 48 hours of giving birth, the female has a fertile postpartum estrus and can become pregnant again if she is kept with a male. Provide the mother with a nest box and nesting material such as unscented tissue paper. A few days before she is due, the mother will make her nest.

The birth usually takes $1^1/_2$ hours, but can range from 30 minutes to 4 hours. Between 6 and 12 young are in a normal litter. An average litter size is eight. The babies are born hairless, and their eyes and ear canals are covered with skin. By the time the pups are one week old, a soft coat of fuzz is discernible. Between 14 and 15 days, their eyes open. At two-and-a-half weeks, they will start to explore the nest, eat solid food, and play-fight with each other. The babies nurse for about 21 days.

Potential Problems

Because mother rats can transmit murine respiratory mycoplasma in utero to their babies, you should never breed infected females or males.

Baby rats at 1 day old (top left), 4 days old (top right), 11 days old (bottom left), and 3 weeks old (bottom right).

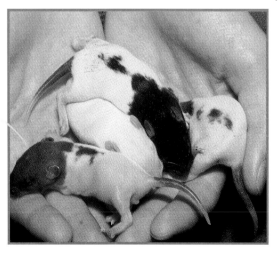